AFTER THE SPRING

AFTER THE SPRING

Economic Transitions in the Arab World

Magdi Amin
Ragui Assaad
Nazar al-Baharna
Kemal Derviş
Raj M. Desai
Navtej S. Dhillon
Ahmed Galal
Hafez Ghanem
Carol Graham
Daniel Kaufmann
Homi Kharas
John Page
Djavad Salehi-Isfahani
Katherine Sierra
Tarik M. Yousef

OXFORD
UNIVERSITY PRESS

OXFORD
UNIVERSITY PRESS

Oxford University Press, Inc., publishes works that further
Oxford University's objective of excellence
in research, scholarship, and education.

Oxford New York
Auckland   Cape Town   Dar es Salaam   Hong Kong   Karachi
Kuala Lumpur   Madrid   Melbourne   Mexico City   Nairobi
New Delhi   Shanghai   Taipei   Toronto

With offices in
Argentina   Austria   Brazil   Chile   Czech Republic   France   Greece
Guatemala   Hungary   Italy   Japan   Poland   Portugal   Singapore
South Korea   Switzerland   Thailand   Turkey   Ukraine   Vietnam

Copyright © 2012 by Oxford University Press

Published by Oxford University Press, Inc.
198 Madison Avenue, New York, New York 10016
www.oup.com

Oxford is a registered trademark of Oxford University Press

Library of Congress Cataloging-in-Publication Data

After the spring : economic transitions in the Arab world / Magdi Amin ... [et al.].
         p. cm.
Includes index.
ISBN 978-0-19-992492-9 (cloth : alk. paper)   1. Arab countries—Economic
policy—21st century.   2. Arab countries—Politics and
government—21st century. 3. Arab countries—Commerce.
I. Amin, Magdi.
HC498.A643 2012
330.917'4927—dc23
2011045961

1 3 5 7 9 8 6 4 2

Printed in the United States of America
on acid-free paper

CONTENTS

PREFACE

The ongoing transitions in the Arab world are among the most dramatic events since the collapse of communism in Eastern Europe. But months after the events in Tunisia that began the Arab Spring in December 2010, it seemed that the bulk of world's attention remained focused on the usual mix of global security, regional politics, and Middle East peace implications of what was transpiring in the Arab world. Underlying economic problems, by contrast, received scant consideration. Seeking to correct this, a few of the authors of the present volume wrote short pieces on employment, labor markets, public services, corruption, and other issues that seemed relevant but ignored in coverage of the Arab Spring.

What was missing, however, was an overall analysis of the central economic reforms needed to sustain the transition. Toward that end, the Global Economy and Development program of the Brookings Institution in Washington, DC, in the summer of 2011, convened a diverse group of scholars, specialists, and former officials to discuss the economic consequences of the Arab Spring, as well as the broader economic imperatives in the region. This jointly authored volume is the outcome of that workshop.

During our discussions, it became clear that the challenges facing the economies of the Arab world—and the economic causes of the Arab Spring—are difficult to segment into separate, self-contained categories. One cannot separate the lack of job creation in Arab economies, for example, from fiscal policies, the investment climate, and demographic structures, just as one cannot separate democratic aspirations from the expectations of Tunisian, Egyptian, Libyan, and Yemeni citizens that changes of government will bring jobs and greater prosperity. Therefore, our approach is to address a series of interrelated issues in an integrated way, with the view that economic and political reforms are the two sides of an Arab social contract that has come under unprecedented stress. We also seek to inform the present transition based on the experience of transitions past—in Eastern Europe, in Latin America, and in Asia—several of which some of us have witnessed at close range.

The transitions in the Arab world are further complicated by the fact that most of these countries have gone through previous reform efforts—including political reform and "structural adjustment"—with varying degrees of success. Rather than listing specific policy reforms, we offer a set of overarching principles by which each government can choose its own approach based on its specific constraints and initial conditions.

Knowing full well that reform agendas must adapt to the dynamics of real-time change, with all its attendant uncertainties, we make no pretense to predict outcomes or to prognosticate on the economic future of the Arab Spring. Indeed, at the time of this writing, the pitfalls of such an exercise are apparent: Libya struggles to establish some sort of postrevolutionary rule of law, Egypt is losing foreign exchange reserves at a rapid pace, and in Cairo's Tahrir Square citizens are once again taking to the streets to press for an advance of democracy rather than a return of what seems to them the old order. Instead, our intentions are relatively modest;

namely, to elevate economic issues on the agenda for the region and to initiate a dialogue between Arab reformers and those around the world who have a stake in events in the Arab world. As a start, this volume benefited from discussions within the region at Cairo University and the Central Bank of Tunisia. We would like to thank the organizers and participants in the seminars we attended there.

This volume has many of its antecedents in the intellectual and financial support of James D. Wolfensohn. Jim turned his longstanding interest in the Middle East into a Middle East Youth Initiative at the Brookings Institution that brought together many of the scholars who contributed to this volume. Their prior research, much of it summarized in the book *Generation in Waiting*, edited by Navtej Dhillon and Tarik Yousef (Brookings Institution Press, 2009), has greatly informed the present volume.

Within Brookings, the project was the brainchild of Kemal Derviş, Vice President for Global Economy and Development, who convened and moderated the June 2011 workshop. Homi Kharas was the leader and main organizer of the summer meetings and prepared the structured requests for input from the participants. Major contributions were received from Magdi Amin (private sector reform), Raj Desai (the state, social contract), Navtej Dhillon (opportunities for young people), and Homi Kharas (regional and global integration). Additional significant contributions were provided by Ragui Assaad (youth, housing, and labor markets), Nazar al-Baharna (civil society, empowerment), Ahmed Galal (national dialogue, development models), Hafez Ghanem (macroeconomics, fiscal sustainability, and subsidies), Carol Graham (well-being), Daniel Kaufmann (governance and institutional quality), John Page (trade and private sector development), Djavad Salehi-Isfahani (education), Kathy Sierra (regional infrastructure), and Tarik Yousef (employment). Raj Desai and Homi Kharas constructed and revised the manuscript from these contributions.

We would like to acknowledge the guidance and financial support of the Swedish Ministry for Foreign Affairs, the Swedish International Development Agency and the German Federal Ministry for Economic Cooperation and Development. Kristina Server at Brookings was responsible for coordinating with these ministries; the authors are grateful for her efforts. We also thank Annick Ducher for her help in facilitating the convening of the workshop and communication between authors. Soumya Chattopadhyay, Karim Foda, Natasha Ledlie, and Veronika Penciakova provided able research assistance for various parts of the volume. Natasha Ledlie, in particular, helped in all aspects of drafting the final manuscript and in ensuring accuracy and consistency. Mary Kraetsch provided the index.

We thank our editors at Oxford University Press, Terry Vaughn and Catherine Rae, for their patience and for accommodating our numerous requests. We are also grateful for the professionalism of Oxford's production team led by Amy Whitmer, and their associates at Newgen, who shepherded our manuscript through to print.

Finally, our work benefited from informal interaction with many of our colleagues at Brookings and from the overall environment conducive to impartial policy-oriented research that Brookings nurtures.

Chapter 1

Introduction

The sweeping changes in the Arab world[1] that began in December 2010 are perhaps the most important transitions of the early twenty-first century. It is tempting to ascribe the Arab Spring to high levels of unemployment, especially among youth, and the suppression of political options, but that seems to be too narrow an explanation because in countries such as Egypt the available evidence showed gradual improvement in these indicators. By the end of 2010, unemployment in the region had modestly declined, though from high levels. Democratic reforms were taking place, albeit in a slow and incremental fashion, and young people had a more optimistic outlook on their economic prospects than the elderly. Along with sound economic growth and increasing foreign direct investment, these trends created a false sense of complacency among policy makers over the pace and impact of progress.

What was missed were other catalysts of growing discontent: the popular perception of entrenched and rising corruption, severely restricted options for participation and representation in policymaking, and failing public services—what might be called a growing governance deficit. Many workers were forced into low-quality jobs in the informal sector, and women, in particular, were

---

1 We define the Arab region to include the countries of North Africa (Algeria, Egypt, Libya, Morocco, and Tunisia), the Arab Levantine states (Jordan, Lebanon, Syria, and the Palestinian Territories), the Arabian peninsular countries (Bahrain, Kuwait, Oman, Qatar, Saudi Arabia, United Arab Emirates, and Yemen), and Iraq.

underrepresented in the labor force, so the share of the population describing themselves as "thriving," an average of current and expected future living standards, was low and falling, creating social and economic deficits. In sum, the Arab Spring was sparked by homegrown movements over dignity, fairness, and exclusion.

Most successful transitions involve simultaneous political and economic reform, and this is likely to be the case for Arab countries as well. Already, a political transition away from autocratic, strong-man rule has begun in Egypt, Libya, and Tunisia, while constitutional reforms have been introduced or promised in Morocco, Jordan, and some Persian Gulf countries. Much has been written about these political reforms and their implications and future trajectories, but there has been less focus on the economic transitions that will be required for democracy to succeed or about how the international community can help. That is unfortunate as Arab public opinion in the initial transition considers better and fairer economic outcomes as important as well-functioning democracy (Figure 1.1).

This volume is aimed at contributing to the discourse on the new economic transitions in the Arab world. There are no ready-made solutions to offer, but it is useful to pose some questions, to propose a set of guidelines for reformers, to focus the debates, and to reflect on the lessons and experiences of recent economic transitions in other countries.

REMAKING THE ARAB ECONOMIES

There remains significant resentment against the forces that supported and perpetuated the old regimes—the businessmen who profited from their connections to rulers, the international financial institutions and aid agencies that provided ever-larger funding

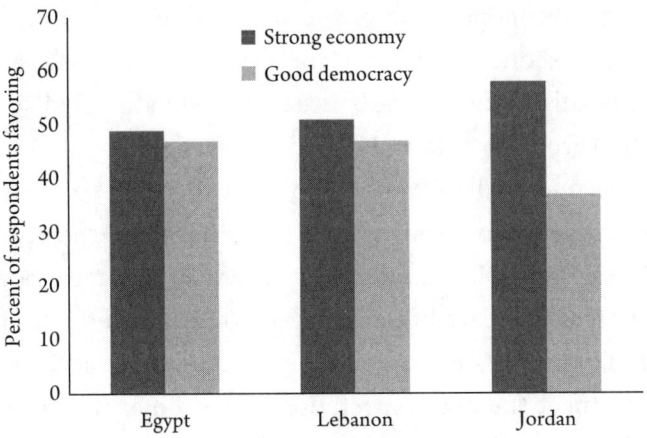

Figure 1.1. Which Is More Important? Strong Economy versus Good Democracy.
(*Source:* Pew Research Center. *Arab Spring Fails to Improve US Image*. Washington, DC: Global Attitudes Project, 2011.)

to the old regimes, and the ruling elites themselves. Yet these were also the forces propelling the economy . New engines of development and a new framework for a discussion of key economic issues are needed.

Getting Started

Transition countries confront three major challenges. First, domestic politics is creating a new nationalism, grounded in a justified sense of self-determination and a desire for solidarity. When nationalism last spread through the Arab world, a particular developmental model based on protection, planning, and patrimony was put in place. That model relied too much on rents rather than production, and on cronyism rather than inclusion. When Arab countries reformed—as they did in the 1990s—they did so half-heartedly and in ways that enriched a small ruling elite. These failures have tainted the very idea of market transitions in Arab states. Support

3

for a strong economic role of the state still exists today, but the political and economic circumstances have changed. There is often not enough distinction made between the regulatory, redistributive and actual producer role of the state.

The second challenge is how to meet soaring expectations for improvements in living standards, at a time when the economies face risks of instability and slower growth. Short-term economic growth prospects have been damaged—tourism, retail trade, construction, housing, financial services, and investment have all suffered. To meet the new expectations, policy makers will need to put in place strategies that help jump-start and sustain economic growth, in a fair and inclusive way.

So far, economic crisis has been averted in the Arab transition countries. The economies of Egypt and Tunisia are projected by domestic and international financial institutions to continue to grow in the short and medium terms, although at a slower pace than before. If these projections come true, it would be the exception rather than the rule for democratic transitions. There have been 103 cases worldwide of a strong shift toward democracy since 1960, and about half of these countries experienced an economic contraction the first year after the transition while 40 percent experienced a contraction lasting at least five years.

Avoiding a contraction and realizing the full growth potential in the Arab world will require significant and broad-based economic reform as well as active policies in some areas, notably in regard to youth, industrial policy, and large infrastructure investments. The current set of economic policies has delivered very low rates of growth of labor productivity and limited formal employment. It has also widened the gap between the superrich and the rest of society and the gap between a large, but shrinking, group that receives public benefits in the form of jobs and subsidies for food, fuel and housing, and growing segments of the population that are excluded from these traditional forms of social welfare because governments have had to ration benefits to affordable, albeit not sustainable, levels.

The third challenge is how to develop a constructive engagement with the regional and global economy, just at a time when the international community is distracted and dealing with the worst years of economic growth since the Great Depression. An outstanding issue is how much the current political transitions will transform the neighborhood compared to how much the neighborhood will affect the ongoing transitions. Arab economies are less well integrated into the global economy or their regional neighborhood than other areas of the world are. Nonoil Arab exports are less than 1 percent of global trade. Intraregional trade is among the lowest in the world. Yet there is a commonality to Arab history, language, and culture so it is reasonable to suppose that there is a regional identity that should not be ignored. Such a view is reinforced by the contagion demonstrated during the Arab Spring and the close links of people, ideas, news carried from country to country, and aspirations across the region.

Moving Forward: Four Needed Economic Transitions

Even though Arab economies are quite heterogeneous in their current endowments of oil, workers, capital, and technology, the broad shape of the economic transitions is clear and common throughout the region. Arab economies have long been dominated by the public sector, and although they have opened a large space for the private sector, this has been achieved in an environment of limited competition, either domestically or from abroad. What has often emerged is a politically favored group, still highly dependent on the state. Large, formal enterprises, owned either by the state or by friends of the state, have failed to provide significant employment growth for the large number of youth entering the labor force. Young people, despite being increasingly better educated, have preferred to wait for a public sector job rather than join the private sector. Many, like the 26-year-old Mohamed Bouazizi, whose self-immolation triggered antigovernment protests in Tunisia, were forced to enter an informal economy with limited prospects for advancement. Migration to other countries has been the only other option.

Low employment growth and low labor productivity growth over many years would have precipitated an economic crisis in many countries, but in the Arab world this has been staved off by the ability of the governments to collect and distribute the proceeds of sizable natural resource rents, largely from oil and gas. Arab countries without natural resources have still benefited from the region's wealth, receiving large worker remittances driven by the high demand for employment in neighboring oil-rich countries.

Without creating employment growth or productivity growth, Arab economies do not have the stable structural features of inclusive economies. In this book, we suggest that four main economic transitions are required.

First, more opportunities for young people need to be created. There are large intergenerational inequities in the distribution of the benefits of economic growth, in favor of a group of public sector employees, elites, and other rent seekers to the disadvantage of the large youth population in the region. The size of the youth base is unprecedented. Almost two-thirds of the population in the Arab world is under the age of 30. Young people are demanding jobs, economic justice, and fairness in economic opportunity and in the distribution of the national resource patrimony. They are ready to participate in creating a new development model, but in many countries their efforts to create active civil society organizations to promote grass roots development have been thwarted by restrictive state regulations. Young people have been discriminated against in terms of budget allocations, have borne the brunt of adjustment during the current transition, and need a major revamp of the educational system to acquire the skills needed to contribute to a competitive economy.

Second, the Arab economies need to modernize their public sectors. There is still a strong demand for a developmental state role in Arab economies and a significant suspicion over the impact of liberal economic reforms that, under the old regimes, served to benefit only a few well-connected private groups. The diagnosis of what is needed in terms of an economic transition is one of eliminating elite capture—the shaping of rules of the game and institutions of the state for the benefit of a few—rather than of a need for fundamental reform of the economic model. In this, the Arab economic transitions differ markedly from economic transitions in eastern Europe where the overall vision of a decisive movement toward a market-oriented economy quickly became a consensus. Instead, in Arab economies, the key reforms in the public sector are likely to be microeconomic, reflecting the process of policymaking (voice and accountability concerns), the effectiveness of government institutions (the quality of the bureaucracy in formulating policies and delivering public services), and the control of corruption.

Most countries in the region have seen deterioration in aggregate economic and political governance compared to the rest of the world over the last decade. Only two Arab countries, Qatar and the United Arab Emirates, saw an improvement in their governance indicators. All other countries had low or severely deteriorating relative indicators of governmental effectiveness, control of corruption, and accountability since 2000.

The third transition is in the private sector. Today, large elements of the private sector are seen as synonymous with corruption. Yet there is no sustainable economic model for the region that does not have the private sector playing a leading role. Governments need to gain the confidence of the private sector and create an environment in which large, medium, and small enterprises are able to operate on a level playing field. That means reducing administrative discretion and petty corruption, simplifying the process of registration, limiting onsite inspections, using information technology solutions to speed up (and promote arms length) tax payments and social insurance contributions, upholding property rights and swift judicial resolution of disputes, strengthening competition policy, and promoting competitive factor markets.

The business community must also regain the confidence of society. Private sector leaders must set aside rent-seeking activities and direct all their energy to production and innovation. They must also embrace social responsibility and philanthropy on a grand scale.

These reforms would have a good chance of yielding immediate benefits if the private sector were already reasonably mature as would be expected in a middle-income economy. However, in Arab countries, there has been a significant failure to industrialize. Manufacturing output per capita is well below international benchmarks for equivalent countries, the share of manufacturing in total output is low, and manufacturing has been declining as a share of gross domestic product (GDP) in Egypt, Morocco, and Tunisia.

Each country faces its own set of challenges. For labor-abundant, low-cost producers like Egypt, the key issue is that the rate at which entrepreneurs create new firms is low—few new entrants have been able to find niches that are globally competitive. For more developed economies like Tunisia, the issue is the rate at which firms are able to transition from lower to higher sophistication in manufacturing, moving up the value chain. For all the Arab economies, the rate of diversification into new products and processes is low.

The oil-rich countries like Libya face different problems. They must develop and create employment despite the problems of Dutch disease that is only likely to worsen if oil prices remain high. In the oil and service sectors, it is more difficult to provide opportunities for learning and developing skills, and technology is increasingly embodied in machines rather than in citizens. Unconventional policies may be necessary, involving substantial subsidies over long periods of time. The new efforts to develop specialized "education cities" and centers of learning and innovation are examples of such policies at work, but their long-term development success is yet to be ascertained.

The fourth economic transition is in the approach to the rest of the world. No successful emerging economy has progressed far without taking advantage of the opportunities provided by global markets and the services provided by global institutions. In some Arab countries, there is a suspicion of the international financial institutions because of the validation and support they provided to the old regimes, even in the face of deteriorating governance. There is a tension between a new nationalism emerging from the political discourse and the need for a constructive engagement with the rest of the world to promote the economic transition.

It will not be easy to resolve this tension, yet it cannot be ignored. For other countries, successful transitions have been helped considerably by the international community. But at present, despite the enormity of the economic challenges faced by Arab economies, the attention of the rest of the world's nations is focused on their own problems. Neither the United States nor Europe have the ability to offer significant grants to smooth the transition, and support in the form of loans adds to public debt and may reduce confidence in the long-term fiscal sustainability of some countries. Grant resources may be available from Gulf countries, but to date these countries have provided limited assistance, and do not offer the kind of technology, management expertise, and connections to the global economy that is needed to really transform Arab economies.

WHAT KIND OF REFORM?

How Fast and How Far?

The association of liberal, market-oriented economic policies with the cronyism and corruption of the old regimes may revive calls for a larger role for the state in the economy and greater regulation of private sector activity. Organized groups, such as public sector workers, may take advantage of newfound freedoms to mobilize and protest to demand significant increases in wages and job protections. Young, educated workers and their families could demand that governments resume the provision of public sector employment to graduates. While populist politicians may feel compelled to respond to these demands, it would undoubtedly come at the expense of young new entrants who would face even slower job growth and greater informality.

There has already been a range of reforms in many Arab economies. Reform matrices have been drawn up and plans presented to bodies such as the G8 in the context of the Deauville Partnership. The list of actions already undertaken is a moving target, but perhaps more important is the narrative emerging from the plans and actions.

Jordan, Syria, and Tunisia have raised allocations for social welfare and cash transfers or extended subsidy payments. Egypt, Jordan, and Syria have increased government salaries and benefits. All these countries have introduced tax breaks, halted scheduled price hikes, or otherwise supported small businesses. The fiscal cost of these programs has varied from 1 to 2 percent of GDP.

Alongside these measures, policy actions in several countries have been taken to improve transparency, support policy debate, and strengthen government efficiency and accountability. The direction of change seems clear. What is at issue is the speed, scope, and sustainability of change. These factors will dictate whether the transitions are permitted to run their course with support from society and business or whether they will be perceived as lacking credibility and engendering instability and dashed expectations.

Countries or Neighborhood in Transition?

It is tempting to suggest that each Arab country should forge its own path in terms of its economic transition independently of one another, but this would be a missed opportunity. Of course, the bulk of the reforms have to be country-specific, but the spillovers between countries, through economic linkages, the contagion of news cycles, the interaction of people, and the sharing of aspirations, are too great to ignore the impact of one country on another. Even Tunisia, perhaps the country that is the most open of all the Arab countries, suffered considerably from the decline in tourist revenues from Libya. Egyptian migrants are to be found throughout the region, and their remittances tie Egypt's economic prospects to those in other countries of the region.

Of course, there is little reason to suppose that full-fledged Arab economic integration is either desirable or practical. No one in the region is likely to give up recently-won sovereignty. A formal Arab union would imply some form of redistribution across countries, and regional politics would not support this at present. But in other instances, regional and international platforms and agreements have played a key role in anchoring economic transitions over the medium term. They have provided a degree of confidence in the reform agenda that is vital for shaping private sector expectations. In their absence, reform programs can be subject to twists and turns linked to domestic politics, and experience elsewhere suggests that these may take a while to settle down.

For the most part, existing agreements with the European Union and the United States have been conducted in a hub-and-spoke fashion, with each Arab country being treated independently.

That permits nations with more advanced economies like Tunisia to move faster and to make use of incentives that link cooperation with progress in economic and political reforms. Yet this hub-and-spoke system avoids encouraging large economies like Egypt to engage more systematically in peer review dialogue with other countries in the region and discourages an environment in which lessons on what is working in different countries can be shared. Given that the region will be experimenting with new models of a developmental state, the scope for learning is likely to be substantial.

The fact that the Arab Spring occured almost simultaneously throughout the Arab world has significance and suggests the existence of an Arab identity that should not be ignored. True, there are huge differences across the region and past efforts to formalize the idea in various regional projects have foundered, but there is an Arab language, a common script, and much common history, literature, music, movies, and architecture. The effort to develop good and feasible policies to deal with what is manifestly a regional challenge is surely a backdrop to national approaches. Cooperative regional projects and the establishment of new regional institutions could be ways of furthering regional solutions in concrete ways. The Arab Spring could prove transformative for the region, but without any regional activities there is a risk that the old structures elsewhere in the region will act to constrain the transition movements.

Economic and Political Transition in Comparative Perspective

The political vacuum at the start of the Arab Spring brings to mind similar periods in other regions—southern Europe in the 1970s, Latin America in the 1980s, eastern Europe in the 1990s—where enormous opportunities for rent seeking, the absence of popular representation, a legal system with irrelevant laws and a weak judiciary, and a multitude of obsolete economic regulations made the task of economic reform all the more intimidating.

There are three propositions that are likely to hold across the Arab world. First, it would be a mistake not to take the opportunity afforded by the major political transition to make significant reforms to the economic structure in each country. Politicians often have a short window of opportunity in which to succeed or fail—what was called the period of "extraordinary politics" when reforms can be accomplished with an ease that will later vanish.[2] Under these conditions, the reformer's objective is to reform before opponents are able to mobilize in order to increase the likelihood of winning reform battles, but also to ensure that reforms are irreversible.

Moreover, the experiences of Russia, of the Philippines after Ferdinand Marcos, and many other cases show that when political change is not accompanied by widespread economic change, there is a risk of reversion on the political front, as old vested interests regain control over the political process through their dominance of the economy, or else of economic stagnation as the power-politics game creates blocking coalitions against change. When old economic structures are preserved or only modestly adapted, it cannot be expected that different outcomes on growth and equity will result.

Since 1960, there have been 103 cases of a major transition toward democracy.[3] These transitions have occurred in all regions, for all income categories, and some transitions have progressed while others stalled. In 57 of these cases, there was a successful

2 Leszek Balcerowicz, (1994), "Understanding Postcommunist Transitions," *Journal of Democracy* 5 (4): 75–89.

3 A major change toward democracy is defined as an increase in the polity indicator of three points or more in a year (the Polity scale goes from negative ten to positive ten).

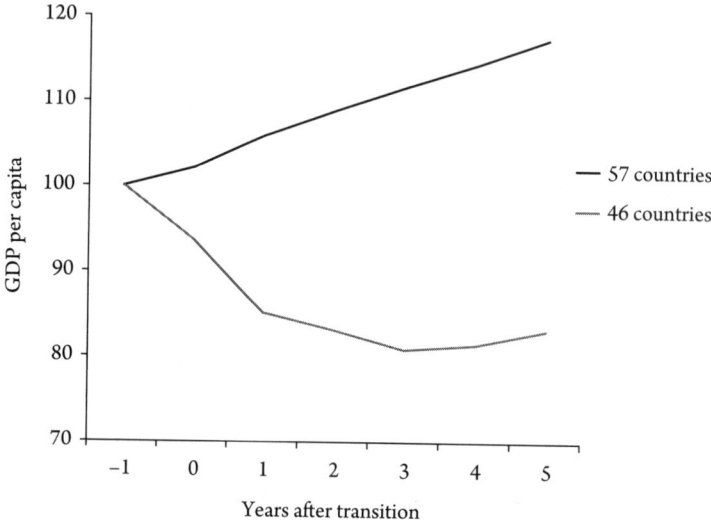

GDP per capita

— 57 countries
— 46 countries

Years after transition

Figure 1.2. Which Path Forward for the Arab Transitions? (*Source:* World Bank. *World Development Indicators,* http://data.worldbankorg/indicator; Integrated Network for Societal Conflict Research. *Polity IV Annual Time-Series 1800–2010.*)

economic transition in the sense that GDP per capita continued to grow steadily over time (Figure 1.2). In 46 cases, there was a sharp decline in GDP per capita compared to the precrisis year. After five years, the cumulative difference between the average of successful and unsuccessful economic transitions was about 35 percent. Getting the economic transition right clearly has enormous benefits.

Some urgency is needed to build a foundation for a successful economic transition in the region. Although international and domestic analysts continue to forecast positive growth trajectories, significant risks remain. In some cases, these may not manifest themselves until later. For example, during the East Asian crisis, turmoil in Thailand did not spread to Indonesia for several months and the Indonesian authorities were quite sanguine about their ability to avoid a crisis of their own even in the fall of 1997. But crises tend to have tipping points that are unpredictable—when confidence falls, the ability of the authorities to stem the tide of capital outflows can be limited. No Arab country has yet reached this tipping point, but the danger should not be discounted. Any such crisis would have far-reaching and potentially damaging effects on both the economic and political transitions under way, so it is imperative to shape a strategy from now that clearly builds confidence within the private sector and that is inclusive of all groups in society. Complacency over the economic situation, or a strategy of waiting for maturation of the political process before embarking on a new economic strategy, could be risky. Yet, a review of the budget documents of the major Arab economies does not indicate a major departure from "business as usual" economic policies.

Second, the four key transitions previously identified must be addressed in a holistic way by framing a broad, long-term economic strategy that creates expectations that growth, fairness, equity, and economic justice will play major roles in the transition to a new economy. In deciding on the priorities of the reform strategy, it may be tempting to try and redress social grievances and injustices first, given the recent history of exclusion of many groups, but although such reforms are urgent and necessary, they may not be sufficient and could even undermine confidence if not accompanied by growth-enhancing reforms. At the end of the day, the economic transition will be about rebuilding the state and improving its institutions—redefining its role, improving voice and accountability, embracing inclusion, and making government bureaucracy more effective.

Third, no reform can be sustained without a guiding vision as to the end point. This has still to emerge from national dialogues. Big questions for Arab countries and their friends in the international community remain unanswered. Is the European approach of incentives for movement toward a liberal, democratic model the right way to go? Or does a regional discourse like the New Partnership for Africa's Development, adopted by the African Union, provide a better way of establishing a comprehensive overall vision around which international support can be mobilized? Are there other models?

Without this overall vision, the extreme duality between oil-rich and other countries in the Arab world interacting with a strong common Arab identity could prove to be a combustible mix. Economic progress in the oil-poor, densely populated countries is in the enlightened self-interest of the region as a whole. The problems of the poorer states cannot be ignored.

Unlike in eastern Europe, there are no simple and ideological solutions that are likely to have popular appeal. Market liberalization, privatization, and laissez-faire solutions with minimal government have been tried in the past, albeit in distorted and incomplete ways, and have failed to deliver fair and equitable outcomes. Equally, an overly state-run approach has failed to deliver jobs or growth. A new Arab generation is emerging that is more pragmatic, that sees opportunities in global markets, new technologies, and private initiative. They are likely to look at a wide menu of options, mixing different approaches: private banks combined with state-run development banks modeled on the Brazilian national development bank, BNDES; private enterprises coupled with successful and efficient state-run firms like Turkish Airlines; private universities competing with state-run universities to create skills for the new economies; tripartite wage negotiations as in Germany. These examples of eclectic, pragmatic choices based on what has worked in other parts of the world will have to be discussed widely with the private sector and civil society and carefully monitored in terms of the results being achieved when applied to Arab economies. By being "militant" about this pragmatism, Arab policy leaders might succeed in developing a sense of national initiative and pride, rather than a feeling that they are asking their countries to follow a particular "foreign" ideology or influence.

NEW TRANSITIONS, NEW DIRECTIONS: OUTLINE OF THE VOLUME

In the remainder of this book we elaborate on the needed transitions based on experiences with transitions in other international contexts as well as the conditions facing the economies in the region. Given the fluidity of the situation in the early stages of transition, it is clear that it would be folly to be overly prescriptive. In fact, experience of other international economic transitions suggests that much of the impact of reforms will depend on the way in which they shape expectations as to the future, so it is likely that different reform strategies and sequences will emerge in each country and will change over time as these expectations shift.

Understanding the Origins of the Arab Spring

The origins of the uprisings in part stem from a dual failure, one political and one economic. For too long authoritarian regimes relied on economic and political institutions to preserve the status quo, creating unsustainable tradeoffs between economic and political freedoms, especially for young people. There was economic growth, but it was not widely shared; there was redistribution but growing corruption. In the end, decades of slow and piecemeal reforms could not prevent the eventual unraveling of the Arab social contract and unmaking of the Arab polity. Chapter 2 explores the proximate sources of the uprisings in the Arab world and explains how the legacies of Arab political development will shape the possibilities for economic reform.

Two pillars of the typical Arab economy have historically allowed rulers to secure the loyalty of their subjects: government jobs and a generous welfare state. In return for these things, Arab citizens were willing to tolerate political restrictions—on civic associations, on access to and representation in government, and on the ability to participate in democratic life. In times of distress and unable to fulfill the economic side of the bargain, Arab rulers have occasionally turned to partial political liberalization. Facing falling oil prices in the 1990s, for example, several countries permitted greater freedom and took steps to allow opposition figures to campaign freely, as long as they did not threaten the regime itself. At the same time, they attempted to increase salaries for civil servants or members of the military or food, fuel, and housing subsidies.

For decades, citizens willingly accepted this authoritarian bargain. It is hard to imagine now, but in the 1960s and 1970s the economies of the Middle East were among the fastest growing in the world—alongside the East Asian "tigers." Unemployment was low, and employment and household incomes were each expanding rapidly. Middle Easterners easily found high-wage work, both at home and especially in the booming oil fields of the Gulf. University-educated Middle Easterners were guaranteed jobs in the public sector. Oil revenues played a pivotal role in sustaining the social contract in both exporting and nonexporting Arab states. For oil producers, oil revenues permitted the creation of vast welfare states. For non–oil producers, remittance income boosted household consumption, especially in rural areas. Loans, grants, and other forms of assistance from oil-producing states to non–oil producers boosted government revenues and sustained redistributive commitments. As late as the early 1980s, job opportunities had grown so fast that Egypt, Tunisia, and Algeria were each reporting labor shortages. Today in these same countries jobs have disappeared, particularly for young people. These economies now suffer some of the highest unemployment rates in the world, and where standards of living were once rising rapidly they are now declining or stagnant.

Expanding Opportunities for Youth

Opportunities for young people must be better addressed. As examined in chapter 3, the share of youth to total population in Arab countries is unprecedented, and the economic and social costs of their current predicament are enormous—joblessness, late marriage, a lack of work experience, delayed household formation, and a loss of self-respect are symptoms of the crisis. Young people have borne the brunt of the economic adjustments to date because most reforms have grandfathered protections to those already receiving benefits. Continuing with that process of incremental reform may be too risky and costly in the current context in which the expectations of young people are high.

This chapter argues that a youth-oriented strategy ultimately depends on a major overhaul of the education system, away from a "credentialist" system that sorts students to make it easier for the best and the brightest to get favored government jobs toward a system that rewards the accumulation of market-relevant skills. Despite ample resources being spent on education, student test scores in the Arab world are poor by international standards, even when correcting for income level. Naturally, educational reform must be conceived as a long-term program. It would require parallel reforms in civil service recruitment and compensation practices, labor market reform, the development of a stronger private sector, curriculum reform, and a change in the mind-set of families and students away from their current strongly expressed preference for a government job.

Paradoxically, public employment guarantees and a meritocratic examination system for the civil service—intended to generate an inclusive, fair outcomes for all students—have resulted in highly unequal opportunities for young people. In order to get into the best universities and do well, families are spending large sums on private tuition. Those who cannot afford this have far less chance at securing a government job. Class, gender, and spatial inequalities are higher than ever before. Addressing these issues is a generational challenge, but the youth issue is so significant that proactive policies may be needed in the short term to complement long-term changes.

Building a Modern State

Chapter 4 looks at the need to modernize the Arab public sector. In some countries, a short-term priority is to stabilize the economy and place public debt dynamics on a sustainable basis. That is not easy because the drivers of public debt dynamics are highly uncertain. The underlying structural public sector deficit may be disguised by the fact that exchange rates may not be sustainable, so the level of the deficit, the key basis for policymaking, cannot be easily ascertained. Budget deficits in Arab countries also do not include any provision for contingent liabilities that may arise in state-owned enterprises or in the banking sector during a transition. The large public subsidies on food and fuel must also be reduced, and targeting improved. Finally, growth prospects are highly uncertain. With so many variables at play, it will not be easy for some countries to develop a macroeconomic program that ensures long-term fiscal sustainability and creates the confidence necessary to attract investors back into their economies.

At one level, Arab debt and deficits are of less immediate concern than in other developing countries, because a considerable portion of the debt is domestic. As a result, the Arab economies do not suffer from what economists have called original sin—a dependency on external debt to fund domestic investments. However, long-term studies of sovereign default show that this does not reduce the probability or cost of default: Historically, domestic debt defaults are as common as external debt defaults, and the costs in terms of output loss and inflation are even more severe when domestic defaults occur. The key issue is the level rather than the composition of debt. Thus, despite the temptation to try and offset the costs of transition with more public spending funded domestically, as is being done currently in Egypt, there may also be a case for a much more cautious stance on fiscal policy.

A long-term challenge for all governments in the region is to deal with the cost and overstaffing of public agencies, and to do so in the context of high unemployment. In the long term, civil service reform must be linked with broader labor market reform, including the provision of unemployment insurance so that there are automatic mechanisms for reducing the costs to individuals of retrenchment from the public sector.

A large public sector has been the key to the survival of Arab governments. Prior to the events beginning in December 2010, the region was home to some of the longest-lived autocratic governments. After independence, Arab countries developed reasonably effective government institutions by global standards. By 2010, many of these same institutions, particularly the economic bureaucracy (state enterprises and line ministries) were being used to reward key constituencies and factions. These networks of privilege eroded the efficiency of the public sector and contributed to corruption. Of course, the degree and character of this corruption vary across countries and agencies, and careful diagnosis will be needed to help reformers prioritize their efforts to rebuild state institutions and to improve the delivery of vital public services.

As an example, there is preliminary evidence to suggest that affordable housing, rubbish collection and sanitation, and to a lesser extent public transport are key areas where public service efficiency has deteriorated in Egypt. In Tunisia, housing, roads, and health care stand out as services in decline. The available data is not robust enough to recommend that the authorities focus on these sectors, but it does suggest that reforms could be crafted on the basis of evidence from citizen feedback, focused in some sectors, and complemented by such cross-cutting institutional improvements as anticorruption measures, transparency, and strengthened voice and accountability processes.

Transforming the Private Business Sector

In chapter 5, we turn our attention to the problems of the private sector. The energies of the Arab businesses need to shift from rent seeking to competitive production. No economy has successfully grown without a strong private sector, but equally the private sector is not a panacea and is seen in some quarters as part of the problem not the solution. Small and medium enterprises and large enterprises have equally important, although somewhat different, roles to play. There is a large small and medium enterprise (SME) sector in the region, but it tends to be informal, lacks global competitiveness, does not export, and has low productivity growth. It is not sufficiently linked into value chains and suffers from lack of access to finance and to good infrastructure.

Large enterprises have higher productivity and good access to financial services but have operated in an uncompetitive environment. They benefited from high levels of effective protection provided through trade policy (tariffs and nontariff barriers) and, importantly, by access to inputs (land, fuel, and credits) at subsidized rates. Recently, even the large business sector tended to push its labor force into informality, as labor laws were increasingly relaxed or simply unenforced. In all countries of the region, the result is a share of manufacturing in GDP that is half the average for comparable countries at a similar stage of development.

Past partial efforts at liberalization and encouragement of the private sector did not have as large a supply response as policy makers expected. Partly, this is because Arab economies are quite heterogeneous and face different challenges that call for different solutions and, partly, because of the lack of credibility that previous reform efforts would be sustained and generalized. As a consequence, simple-minded application of "liberalize and privatize" approaches will not work across the region. More nuanced and differentiated approaches are called for.

Some economies, like Egypt and Morocco, have yet to find dynamic, competitive mass products—they need to "break in" to world markets and might focus on task-based trade and agroindustry. Their focus should be on export processing zones, attraction of foreign direct investment, and employee skills. Other economies, like Tunisia and Lebanon, face the challenge of mastering more sophisticated products and tasks, moving up the value chain and improving quality and timeliness. Spatial policies, logistics, skills, and the regulatory environment are critical. Last, richer oil producers, like Algeria, Libya, and the Gulf Cooperation Council countries, need to diversify by finding niche markets in high value-added manufacturing and services. The keys for them: innovation and human capital development.

The agenda for private sector reform is enormous. Most have a complex, overburdened structure of administrative controls. For example, Egypt has cataloged 36,000 regulations affecting the private sector. Many of these regulations operate at cross-purposes, cover different ministries, and are implemented by different levels of government. There is considerable administrative discretion that gives rise to pervasive corruption. Sometimes, even when regulations are removed, bureaucracies continue to implement the old laws. There is limited citizen or business recourse.

Firms find it hard to start a new business and also to close down. In some countries, bankruptcy is considered a crime. That deters innovation, investment and risk taking. More broadly, creditor rights, quality of information, collateral regimes, and other legal rights are unclear and underdeveloped. The Arab world ranks last among all regions in this regard. Partly as a result of this situation, private sector firms often focus on successful rentseeking, rather than production and innovation.

Two parallel tracks for private sector reform could be useful. One track could be to pursue broad-based strategies, focused on greater competition, anticorruption, financial and judicial reform, and labor market reform. That is a long-term endeavor, and the pace and sequencing of reforms will have to be adjusted to fit country circumstances. It is unlikely to deliver quick results, but without some progress on this agenda, the longer-term prospects of the economy would be compromised.

The second track is to develop more focused strategic initiatives around a new active industrial policy. Areas that seem to have some traction in the region include information and communications technology (ICT), tourism, logistics, and education. E-government and the outsourcing of a variety of public services can be a catalyst. This industrial policy should not be confused with old ideas of "picking winners" and supporting them for decades. Instead, it should be understood as a process of joint learning and problem solving between the public and private sectors that can help resolve logistical, information, and institutional problems in a specified time frame.

Better Global and Regional Integration

As suggested in chapter 6, there are several ways in which a more constructive relationship between Arab economies and the rest of the world would help the new economic transitions. External markets, whether regional or global, offer opportunities for rapid economic growth, and much more can be done to take advantage of these. There are already a large number of bilateral and regional free trade agreements with the most important global markets, including some covering the services sectors, so implementing existing agreements, building trust, and harmonizing regional procedures should be the focus of efforts. Tackling nontariff barriers and improving trade-related infrastructure and logistics seem to be priorities.

Another area where regional cooperation can potentially provide economic benefits is through the implementation of large regional infrastructure projects. North Africa is the most attractive location on Earth to develop concentrated solar power. It has large tracts of land where the intensity of solar radiation is very high, and it is close to major consumer markets in Europe. Investments in a regional grid as well as in solar generation would be needed to put this plan into effect, but if it went forward the impact on jobs and exports would be substantial.

In other previous transitions in other parts of the world, the international community has played a valuable role in providing financial resources and anchors to support multiyear reform programs. Such programs help build confidence and shape expectations in a way that crowds in private investments. In the post–Arab Spring world, this may be complicated. The resources available from the international community are largely in the form of loans, not grants, and those are less valuable for countries struggling to maintain fiscal discipline. So far, only a trickle of the promised international financial support has actually been disbursed or taken up by the transition countries.

On the policy front, international institutions must start by building more trust in the region. They are perceived as supporters of the old regimes because their operational modalities have been to support whatever government is in power. In a context of transitional or weak governments, it is important for international institutions to make independent assessments of the likely benefits of reform programs for the majority of the people. Their failure to do so in the past was a mistake from which they should learn.

With the wisdom of hindsight, it is clear that the narrow metrics of economic development, like GDP growth, foreign direct investment, and strength in the balance of payments ignored the signs of worsening corruption, as well as deterioration in institutional effectiveness and well-being. Some of the international financial institutions are less capable and less comfortable with undertaking analysis of corruption, cronyism, and of the potential capture of the state by special interest groups, then basing their cooperation on the results of such analysis. But this is now essential. In the current environment, it would be useful if the international institutions worked more closely with civil society and the emerging, more democratic parliaments.

One contribution that the international community can make is to share lessons of other transition experiences with Arab policy makers, and this has already started. There are many relevant experiences of economic and social transitions, ranging from process issues, such as how to work with civil society and pursue transparency and anticorruption reforms, to policy issues such as decentralization and "charter cities" or industrial zones to such operational schemes as volunteering programs, skills development programs, and first-loss guarantee schemes.

WHAT NEXT? STABILITY, CONFIDENCE, AND CREDIBILITY

Institutional reforms are at the heart of transitions described, but they can involve decades-long processes. The announcement of such reform programs can help build a sense of purpose and confidence, and they can usefully be started through a debate among all stakeholders. That can be done at national and regional levels but should not neglect a dialogue at the local and community level where civil society, small businesses, and individuals can most easily engage with local governments as to their aspirations and priorities. It is important to harness the energy of those who won the revolution into a process to win the transition or risk a backlash of disappointment and frustration.

By themselves, institutional changes are unlikely to deliver substantial and tangible results in the short term; some "low hanging" deliverables through active social and economic programs are needed. These must be sufficient to achieve social stability, business confidence, and credible and sustainable macroeconomic outcomes.

Some countries, like Indonesia, were able to achieve social stability by channeling the energy and imagination of youth and civil society into a range of political, civic, and economic activities through nonprofit organizations and professional associations. Their activities included monitoring of government programs, direct delivery of services, advocacy, and organization using Internet and social media, capacity development and advisory work, and engagement in debate and dialogue. Volunteer activities also blossomed. To make this easier, government policies proved instrumental in providing data and information more easily (transparency), shortening the time period to register as a nongovernmental organization (NGO) or association and reducing regulations on their activities (or ceasing to enforce existing regulations), decentralizing and outsourcing public service delivery, and freeing up access to and use of all kinds of media. Direct government programs of short-term job creation and skills training also helped. Short-term benefits were realized from the activities themselves as well as from the feeling of empowerment and the social stability that was created. Signs of successful implementation of such programs in Tunisia are already evident.

Restoring business confidence is the second short-term imperative. There is a delicate balance to be struck between holding those elements of the previous regime that engaged in corrupt practices accountable and securing confidence in property rights for the future. Large and small businesses must feel confident that it is worthwhile to invest domestically and that opportunities and risks are fairly balanced compared to investments elsewhere in the world. Broad-based reforms will help over time, but in the short term, specific projects and programs and new public-private partnerships can build trust that the private sector will have a prominent role in the economy.

Finally, Arab policy makers need to pay close attention to achieving credible macroeconomic outcomes. There is still a risk that some economies, particularly those with high debt and deficits, may enter a crisis during which they face difficulty in funding fiscal or balance of payments deficits. Cautious borrowing policies with secure financing plans, subsidy reform, and improved government effectiveness in select service delivery areas are short-term priorities that can complement longer-term, broad-based efforts to improve transparency and combat corruption.

In terms of the international community's assistance, one idea is to develop a regional assistance track to complement the country-specific track that is the current basis of development cooperation. A regional approach is appropriate to combat contagion from the viral spread of social consciousness through media and news cycles as well as through economic links of trade, investment, and migration. Because of this, instability anywhere in the region can quickly spread into other countries, so it is in the interests of all countries in the region to promote economic and democratic reforms that have the support of the population. For the international community, the conclusion is that common standards with respect to governance, democracy, and human rights should be applied in their relationships across the Arab world. If not, they can unwittingly contribute to further shocks and instability and again become associated with support of unpopular regimes.

A new regional bank, agency, or platform could prove useful as a mechanism for intermediating between domestic and international political considerations, on the one hand, and economic needs, on the other hand. Such an entity would be uniquely and solely focused on the issues of transition in the Arab world and could play a leading role on trade and logistics facilitation, regional infrastructure financing, and support to the private sector, as well as acting as a portal for bringing relevant experiences from the rest of the world to the region. There are of course existing development institutions that can and are playing such a role, including the Arab League and multilateral institutions, but a new specifically Arab institution by and for Arab countries in transition with an innovative charter and agenda could channel resources and be a source of pride for the dynamic forces of the Arab world. The region lacks good formal evaluation practices or knowledge-sharing platforms to understand better what will work in the Arab context. A regional development platform could provide such expertise and learning in an objective fashion.

The international community must also carefully modulate the speed of its assistance to country circumstances. The economic costs of transition are highest now, so early support is most valuable. Yet moving fast often means moving alone. If the international community does not coordinate its activities and try to exploit synergies, there is considerable risk of overlap and waste. Reformers in countries such as Morocco and Tunisia, where transitions have thus far been less disruptive, may be able to capitalize on windows of opportunity and move rapidly. In Egypt, Libya, and perhaps other countries still engaged in political transitions, however, the situation facing reformers is less clear. The danger is that the political pressures on international agencies to engage might overcome the technocratic imperatives to provide technically sound development assistance.

Good long-term results are more likely to come from partnerships and a deliberate pace of implementation building on evidence of what works. It is likely that the Arab economic transition will be long, with many twists and turns along the way. Pragmatic approaches, coupled with strong diagnostics, can help guide policy along the way.

Chapter 2

The Origins of the Arab Spring

Two interrelated reform failures are at the center of events in the region: one political, one economic. Politically, the failure to develop pluralistic and open systems has left few avenues for citizen participation in civic and political life or for access to and representation in government. That this has occurred despite major accomplishments in health and education over the past decades is one reason for the now outdated notion of Arab exceptionalism.[1] Economically, governments in the region failed to generate inclusive, fair, and equitable growth. As a result, some of the economic benefits to which citizens grew accustomed—public sector employment guarantees and generous welfare benefits—grew to become unaffordable and excluded many young people and other new entrants into the labor force. Arab economies became highly dualistic, with insiders who received benefits from the state and outsiders who did not.

A vast gap emerged between the lavish lifestyles of the ruling families of Egypt, Tunisia, and Libya, along with their cronies, and the common man. The elites, sitting at the critical nodes of the state and of key private segments of the economy, abused formal and informal institutions to control the accumulation and distribution of resources and jobs to perpetuate their power and amass wealth. Monopolized, top-down corruption was an instrument for

---

1 As several observers have noted, the contrast between high rates of human development and the absence of political democracy has historically made the Arab world, in this regard, highly exceptional.

the capture of the polity and economy. In return for loyalty to the ruling elite, associates were provided with jobs (even at lower levels of the public sector) and access to resources. Paradoxically, in countries such as Egypt, the elite's power and hold over political and economic resources expanded even during periods of partial economic liberalization because of the absence of effective domestic or international competition.

THE UNRAVELING ARAB SOCIAL CONTRACT

Following independence, the Arab public sector emerged as the lynchpin of a political-economic system designed to support redistribution and equity in economic and social policy. Its principal features included: agrarian reforms combined with the nationalization of industry, banking, insurance, and trade; the adoption of import substitution and the protection of local industry; a central role for the state in the provision of welfare and social services; and a vision of the political arena, as fundamentally noncompetitive and "organic." This latter component involved significant centralization and government control of political parties, trade unions, professional and civic associations, and other mechanisms for collective political action.

This classic authoritarian bargain—whereby citizens accept political exclusion in exchange for state provision of employment, education, housing, health care, food subsidies, and other benefits—is well known and is by no means exceptional to the Arab world.[2] Central components of the Arab authoritarian bargain are detailed in postindependence basic laws, public policies, and importantly,

---

2 Raj M. Desai, Anders Olofsgård, and Tarik M. Yousef, (2009), "The Logic of the Authoritarian Bargain," *Economics and Politics* 21 (1): 93–125.

in constitutions that address the position of workers as well as the need for states to assume responsibility for providing work and social welfare (Table 2.1).

Among the regulations promulgated were those that mandated job security guarantees as well as relatively high public sector wages with generous nonwage compensation benefits (such as family allowances), alongside prohibitions or sharp restrictions on the dismissal of workers. Such policies were intended to provide economic stability and security to organized labor and to serve as a means of redistribution of collective wealth. However, along with these protections came restrictions on the political activity of labor, including limits on the right to strike.

Governments also moved from regulating private sectors to direct control of production through the nationalization of private assets. In response, public sectors grew to become the dominant employers in Arab states—a legacy that characterizes the region to this date. The International Labor Organization (ILO) estimates that 29 percent of total employment in the Arab world is in the government and public enterprise sectors, twice the global average.[3] Import-substitution strategies also created constraints and incentives that influenced investment and production, with implications for labor demand and job creation. Regulation of agrarian sectors, land reform, and an urban bias in social policy had significant effects on rural labor markets, promoting rapid urbanization and largely eliminating large landowners, previously the most powerful class in many Arab states and the one group potentially capable of serving as a check on bureaucratic and authoritarian excess.[4]

3 International Labour Organization, (2009), *Growth, Employment and Decent Work in the Arab Region: Key Policy Issues* (Beirut: ILO).

4 Joel Beinin, (2001), *Workers and Peasants in the Middle East* (New York: Cambridge University Press).

Table 2.1 RIGHT-TO-WORK PROVISIONS IN ARAB CONSTITUTIONS

Constitution	Article
Algeria (1963)	§ 10 The fundamental objectives of the democratic and popular Algerian Republic are…the guarantee of the right to work.
Algeria (1996)	§ 55 (1) All citizens have a right for work.
Bahrain (1973)	§ 13 (b) The state guarantees the provision of job opportunities for its citizens and the fairness of work conditions.
Bahrain (2002)	§ 13 Work is the duty of every citizen, is required by personal dignity, and is dictated by the public good. Every citizen has the right to work and to choose the type of work within the bounds of public order and decency.
Egypt (1971)	§ 13 Work is a right, a duty, and an honor ensured by the State.
Iraq (1990)	§ 32 (a) Work is a right, which is ensured to be available for every able citizen.
Iraq (2005)	§ 22 (1) Work is a right for all Iraqis in a way that guarantees a dignified life for them.

Jordan (1952)	§ 23 (1) Work is the right of every citizen, and the State shall provide opportunities for work to all citizens by directing the national economy and raising its standards.
Kuwait (1963)	§ 41 (2) Work is a duty of every citizen necessitated by personal dignity and public good. The State shall endeavor to make it available to citizens and to make its terms equitable.
Libya (1969)	§ 4 Work in the Libyan Arab Republic is a right, a duty, and an honor for every able-bodied citizen.
Morocco (1992)	§ 13 All citizens have equal rights to education and to work.
Oman (1996)	§ 12 Every citizen has the right to engage in the work of his choice within the limits of the Law.
Palestinian NA (2003)	§ 25 (1) Work is a right, duty and honor. The Palestinian National Authority shall strive to provide it to any individual capable of performing it.
Saudi Arabia (1993)	§ 28 The State provides job opportunities for whoever is capable of working.
Syria (1973)	§ 36 (1) Work is a right and duty of every citizen. The state undertakes to provide work for all citizens.

(continued)

Table 2.1 (CONTINUED)

Constitution	Article
Tunisia (1959)	Preamble We proclaim that the republican regime constitutes … the most certain way for assuring the protection of the family and guaranteeing to each citizen work, health, and education.
UAE (1971)	§ 20 Society shall esteem work as a cornerstone of its development. It shall endeavor to ensure that employment is available for citizens and to train them so that they are prepared for it.
Yemen (1991)	§ 10 Every citizen has the right to undertake work chosen by him and in accordance with the law.

Source: International Constitutional Law Database.

Oil revenues played a critical role in sustaining this social contract in oil-exporting and nonexporting states alike. For oil producers, oil revenues permitted the creation of vast welfare systems that served as key mechanisms for distributing largesse to citizens (though not to foreign migrant workers). For non–oil producers, emigrants to oil-rich neighbors sent substantial remittances home, boosting household consumption and income, especially in rural areas. Loans, grants, and other forms of assistance from oil-producing states to non–oil producers supported government finances and sustained redistributive commitments. At the peak of the oil boom in the early 1980s, some 3.5 million Arab migrant workers—mainly from Egypt, Jordan, Syria, Lebanon, Yemen, and Morocco—were employed in the oil states of Saudi Arabia and other Gulf states. Oil revenue–fed social systems were particularly popular among public sector employees and other core constituency groups of the elite. For three decades, these groups were the biggest winners from the Arab social contract. Not surprisingly, in countries like Syria, 80 percent of graduates preferred a public sector job.[5]

But the instability of the Arab social contract became increasingly clear by the early 1980s when oil prices began to plummet. By the end of the decade, the strains in the social contract had grown into a major economic crisis.

Falling oil prices in the 1980s cut natural resource revenues as well as demand for migrant labor in oil-rich Arab states and reduced remittance flows. With declining revenues, public sector wage bills and other commitments drove massive increases in public debt in many Arab states. A heavy business regulatory environment impeded the development of export-led sectors and limited

5 Navtej Dhillon and Tarek Yousef, (2009), *Generation in Waiting: The Unfulfilled Promise of Young People in the Middle East* (Washington, DC: Brookings Institution Press).

nonoil, nonremittance foreign exchange earnings. Meanwhile, labor productivity continued to decline, unemployment levels increased and governments faced growing pressure to reform.

The typical macroeconomic reform took the shape of cuts in subsidies, reduced public expenditures, and flexible exchange rate regimes. In a move strongly supported by donors, most Arab governments also embarked on microeconomic structural adjustment, including Algeria, Egypt, Jordan, Morocco, Syria, Tunisia, and the oil exporters of the Arabian Peninsula. Many governments entered international economic institutions, such as the General Agreement on Tariffs and Trade/World Trade Organization (GATT/WTO), and signed bilateral and multilateral trade agreements. By the early 1990s, debt levels declined, inflation was brought under control, and macroeconomic performance was improving.

Economic reforms included many of the elements familiar to Latin America and eastern Europe: privatization of state-owned enterprises, fiscal reform and trade liberalization, deregulation, and the strengthening of the institutional foundations of the market. However, implementation of these measures was uneven, hesitant, and incomplete, characterized by significant cronyism, with politically connected elites enjoying privileged access to land, markets, contracts, finance, and services that resulted from limited market openings. Smaller and newer firms, without privileged access, faced substantial obstacles such that growth was narrowly concentrated and key sectors remained dominated by a few large players.

Partly as a result, the Arab world's economic recovery in the 1990s was generally weak. Most significantly, aggregate labor productivity growth that should have improved with better resource allocation and openness to external markets remained stagnant through the 1990s (Figure 2.1). Only sub-Saharan Africa had lower productivity growth during this period. In the last ten years, productivity growth has ticked up but has increased at an anemic

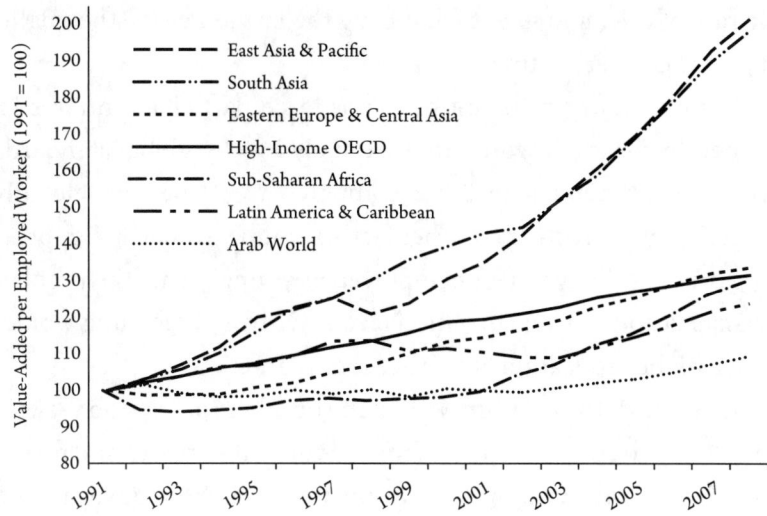

Figure 2.1. Productivity by Region, 1991–2008. (*Source:* World Bank. *World Development Indicators*, http://data.worldbankorg/indicator.)

pace of 1 percent per year. Over the last twenty years, productivity growth in the Arab world has steadily fallen behind that in all other countries and has increased at a pace of only one-tenth the rate of productivity growth in East and South Asia.

Low labor productivity growth may be partly associated with the fact that much of the job creation in the Arab world has been in the informal sector. On average, informal employment (self-employment and working for family without pay) accounted for about 60 percent of total employment in poor Arab countries. A detailed study of Egypt showed that for one-third of the population their first job was in the informal sector in 2005, compared to 15 percent in 1975, while only 30 percent of first-time job seekers found employment in the formal public or private sectors.[6] Thus, although employment itself continued to rise in the Arab world and

6 Ragui Assaad and Ghada Barsoum, (2007), *Youth Exclusion in Egypt: In Search of "Second Chances,"* Middle East Youth Initiative Working Paper (2), Wolfensohn Center for Development and Dubai School of Government. Other categories of first-time work are self-employment and irregular wage employment.

the rate of unemployment fell during the last ten years, the quality of jobs was deteriorating.

Women suffered the most. Labor force participation rates for women in the Arab world are extremely low by global standards, averaging 26 percent in 2008 compared to 52 percent globally. Empirically, correcting for other factors, young women in Egypt are four times as likely to be unemployed as young men.[7] The problem persists despite rising education levels. Only half of young women with a higher education enter the labor market.

Over time, the rapid growth in the numbers of new job seekers, coupled with continued low labor productivity growth and formal employment growth, pressured the ability of Arab governments to continue to maintain universal access to a number of welfare commitments. While earlier generations of youth benefited from free education, public sector job guarantees, subsidized housing, and other benefits, the new generation of those born after 1980 has received little of that, and as a result, their frustrations with the system have been building for more than a decade.

THE LEGACY OF THE ARAB POLITY

Over the last 50 years a pattern has emerged of more government welfare spending and fewer political freedoms when oil prices and general economic conditions were favorable, and less government spending and moves toward political liberalization when oil prices fell and regional economic conditions worsened (Figure 2.2).

It is a mistake to think, however, that the overall picture in 2010 was one of growing instability or greater political oppression. The trends of quantitative indicators of instability in Arab economies

---

7 Op. cit.

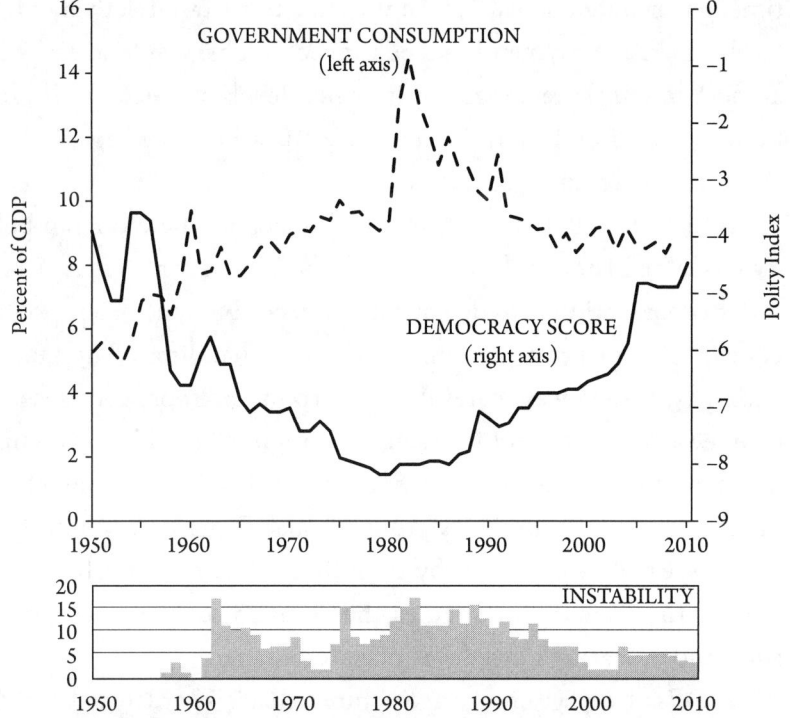

Figure 2.2. Government Spending, Democracy, and Instability in Arab States.
Government consumption is the average percent of GDP weighted by PPP-converted GDP in constant dollars. Democracy score is the unweighted average based on the Polity Index and ranges from −10 (least democratic) to +10 (most democratic). Instability is a cumulative, regional score based on the Political Instability Task Force measure of state failure. (*Sources:* Alan Heston, Robert Summers, and Bettina Aten. Penn World Table, Version 7.0. Center for International Comparisons of Production, Income, and Prices. Philadelphia: University of Pennsylvania, 2011; Monty G. Marshall and Keith Jaggers. Polity IV Project. *Political Regime Characteristics and Transitions, 1800–2010.* College Park: University of Maryland, 2010; Political Instability Task Force. *Internal Wars and Failures of Governance, 1955–2009.* Vienna, VA: Center for Systemic Peace, 2010.)

were actually improving between 2003 and 2010. Several governments embarked on a series of tactical political openings, and their polity score—a measure of democracy—got better, but in all cases, the reforms relied on organizations closely tied to incumbents (political parties, the military and security apparatus) to ensure that rival political forces were restrained and co-opted. At the same time, government consumption was able to sustain relatively high levels of welfare payments and public sector jobs. While still highly autocratic and characterized by immense levels of executive discretion, the Arab polities in December 2010 were more "open" than those of the previous generation.[8]

While ultimately transitional and unstable, the old Arab polity has left a historical legacy that will endure in three areas. First, many organizations are deinstitutionalized. Bureaucracies, political parties, legislatures, and militaries have had limited delegated authority. Rulers were careful to constrain any room for those in charge of these bodies to threaten the regime, unwilling to relinquish ultimate control. They did this by fashioning competing organizations—paramilitary groups, "palace" guards, and multiple factions, each presided over by an individual with overarching loyalties to the ruler. In these bodies, the formation of codified internal rules and operating procedures was discouraged.

The disadvantage of such a structure is that it is hard to make credible long-term commitments to investors and citizens beyond a narrow circle of favored groups.[9] This absence of a strong institutional structure may be one of the reasons for the lack of a supply-side response to the partial economic reforms that had taken place before 2010.

Second, groups that were not part of the favored circle were systematically excluded from sharing economic benefits. Most Arab economies are characterized by rising inequality, including

---

8 Of course, the process of gradual political liberalization has been uneven, leaving the Gulf Cooperation Council (GCC) states (with the possible exception of Kuwait) unaffected by this trend. Even in Egypt, Jordan, Morocco, and Algeria, the pattern was characterized by steps forward and backward: "When pressure mounts, both from within the society and from outside, the regime loosens its constraints and allows more civic activity and a more open electoral arena—until political opposition appears as if it may grow too serious and effective." Larry Diamond, (2010), "Why Are There No Arab Democracies?" *Journal of Democracy* 21 (1): 93–104.

9 For a review, see Scott Gehlbach and Philip Keefer, (2011), "Investment Without Democracy: Ruling-Party Institutionalization and Credible Commitment in Autocracies," *Journal of Comparative Economics* 39 (2): 123–139.

a widening gap between urban and rural residents, adults and the young, and between the benefits and privileges granted to a shrinking portion of public sector workers and all others. This exclusion contrasts with public expectations that the state is responsible for all its citizens' development and prosperity, through a combination of public sector employment and subsidies. Despite waiting lists that stretch up to 13 years, large percentages of Arab populations prefer government jobs to employment in the private sector. Even among Arab youth, in most countries large pluralities express preferences for government jobs over other types of employment.[10] The inevitable frustrations borne from long stretches of unemployment exacerbate feelings of economic insecurity for many even as it raises the social and political costs of reform.

Third, natural constituencies in favor of economic reform— private sector workers, smaller entrepreneurs, women, youth, and other segments of civil society—were deprived of a platform for genuine representation in policymaking. As shown in Figure 2.3, regional economies were generally subpar in indicators of "voice and accountability" and had mostly seen significant deterioration in performance relative to the rest of the world (with the exception of Turkey) between 2000 and 2009. The military and business groups that had posed credible challenges to ruling elites in previous decades were co-opted to support Arab rulers. The merchant class that in other societies has been a natural advocate of a limited, constrained executive did not play a strong role in the change in Arab economies, preferring to enter alliances through which they received a portion of the economic rents and other benefits that the state distributed. Business and professional associations

---

10 The exceptions are Lebanon, Algeria, and Morocco. In these countries, the preference is for self-employment, followed by public sector employment, then private sector employment. In no Arab country do youth prefer private sector employment over the public sector. See Silatech and the Gallup Organization, (2009), *The Silatech Index: Voices of Young Arabs.*

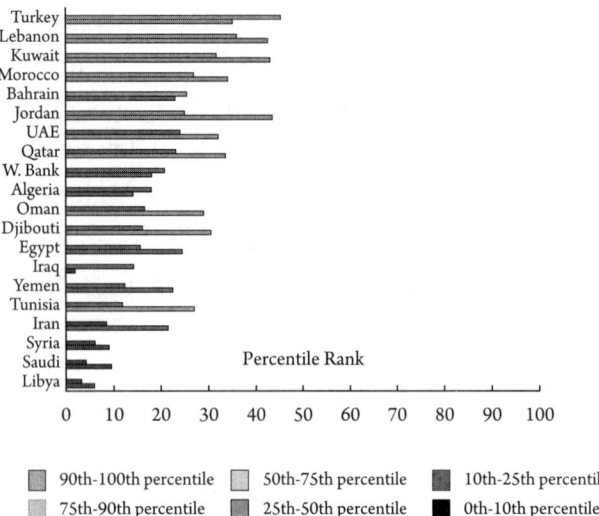

Figure 2.3. Voice and Accountability in the Middle Eastern and North African Countries. Note that for each country the bottom bar exhibits the initial period, 2000, and the top bar exhibits 2009. (*Source:* D. Kaufmann, A. Kraay, and M. Mastruzzi. *Worldwide Governance Indicators: A Summary of Data, Methodology and Analytical Issues.* Worldwide Governance Indicators Project, 2010, available at www.govindicators.org.)

and trade unions, which have prodded reforms in other countries, are described as weak, unrepresentative, or captured in the Arab world.[11]

PARTIAL REFORM AND INTERNATIONAL EXPERIENCES

The partial quality of economic policy reform—more progress on exchange rate stabilization than on privatization, more progress on fiscal policy reform than on the liberalization of labor markets—can be understood as a product of the embedded nature of the

11 World Bank, (2009), *From Privilege to Competition: Unlocking Private-Led Growth in the Middle East and North Africa* (Washington, DC: World Bank), pp. 187–189.

interventionist-redistributive social contract in the Arab world. For example, institutional arrangements created to link organized labor and the state became mechanisms through which privatization was resisted.[12] Governments faced political and social constraints in their attempts to reduce welfare expenditures. Memories of violent mass protests against austerity measures, such as those that took place in Tunisia in 1984, in Morocco in 1981, and in Egypt in 1977, made strong welfare reform into a taboo, even 20 years later.[13]

An alternative (and easier) approach to reform was to reduce enforcement. For example, there appears to have been a tacit agreement between the political and business elites in Egypt that labor laws need not be strictly applied to new employees. Thus, the growing informalization of labor markets spread beyond self-employment and employment in small businesses to include unregulated employment in the formal private sector.

Moreover, partial reforms created opportunities for business and political elites to increase their rent-seeking activities. Prereform networks, as in other regions of the world, had proved extremely resilient in Arab states. Many of the beneficiaries of these networks of privilege were able to arbitrage between liberalized and nonliberalized parts of the economy, continuing to receive subsidies at home in the form of cheap credit or inputs with controlled prices, while obtaining new profits due to an expansion in global market access—much in the same way that Russian "oligarchs" prospered in the 1990s.[14] The concentration of economic gains generated by

12 Marsha P. Posusney, (1997), *Labor and the State in Egypt: Workers, Unions, and Economic Restructuring* (New York: Columbia University Press).

13 Iliya Harik and Denis J. Sullivan, (1992), *Privatization and Liberalization in the Middle East* (Bloomington: Indiana University Press).

14 Steven Heydemann shows that the level and dispersion of effective protection rates across industries in Egypt was more heavily influenced by energy pricing policies than by external tariffs. See Heydemann (2004), "Networks of Privilege: Rethinking the Politics of Economic Reform," in *Networks of Privilege in the Middle East* (New York: Palgrave Macmillan); World Bank, (2011), *A Profile of Border Protection in Egypt: an Effective Rate of Protection Approach Adjusting for Energy Subsidies* (Washington, DC: World Bank).

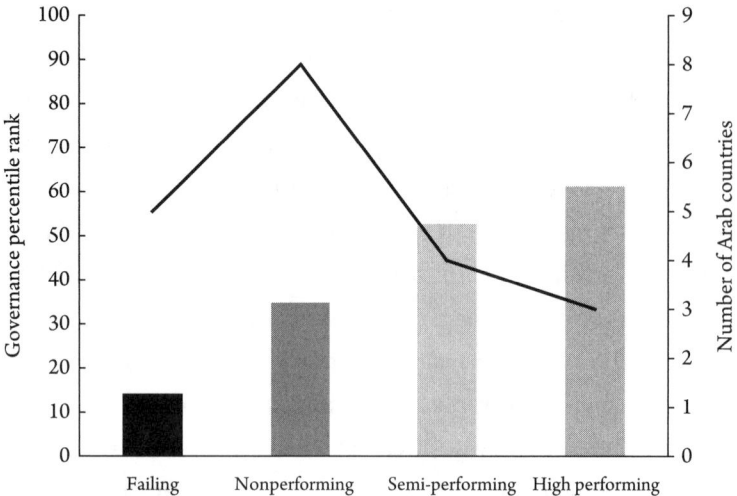

Figure 2.4. Governance Performance Groupings in the Middle Eastern and North African Countries, 2009. This graph shows the average of voice and democratic accountability, government effectiveness, and control of corruption, for four groups of countries. (*Source:* D. Kaufmann, A. Kraay, and M. Mastruzzi. *Worldwide Governance Indicators: A Summary of Data, Methodology and Analytical Issues.* Worldwide Governance Indicators Project, 2010, available at www.govindicators.org.)

selective policy reforms in the hands of those with established ties to governments did as much to undermine their legitimacy among Arab populations as any real-sector effects of reform.

Where did these partial reforms leave Arab countries in 2009, prior to the uprisings? It is hard to generalize, even though on average overall governance in the region is poor and there are few good governance performers. Governance has many different political, economic, and institutional dimensions, but if just one indicator from each of these dimensions is considered and averaged into a composite aggregate, it appears that four different governance groups emerge in the Arab world (Figure 2.4).

A "top group" of the countries—Qatar, the United Arab Emirates, and Turkey—can be classified as "relative performers" implying they are above the median for the world as a whole (averaging around the 60th percentile). Within this group, governance more broadly has improved over the last decade by an average of 6 percentage points over the selected indicators.

The second group of "semiperformers" comprises four countries—Kuwait, Bahrain, Oman, and Jordan—rating at around the 50th percentile worldwide. All these countries underwent severe deterioration during the past decade, although their level of governance performance was average for the world. The third and lower-performing group ("nonperformers") is the largest group and comprises eight countries, rating below two-thirds of the world on average. These countries also witnessed a slight deterioration in governance performance, although because the level was already low, they did not experience the same degree of decline as the semi-performers. The last group, "failing," comprises five countries, with countries rating around the bottom decile worldwide and experiencing deteriorating governance during the past decade.

This classification of countries in the region makes it clear that different countries have different initial political and institutional conditions and face different priorities for reform. Each will have to choose its own path forward. Countries differ for other reasons, such as ethnoreligious fractures and the presence or absence of a professional army, civil service, and other basic state institutions. In rich and nonreforming monarchies, it remains to be seen how long they can appease their citizens with increasing payoffs while suppressing dissent.

It is also important to recognize the different governance priorities within a country. Just taking one example, the control of corruption, the data suggest that this differs quite markedly across institutions. For example, as shown in Figure 2.5, Egypt's priorities in the fight against corruption appear to be in captured policies and budgetary leakages (while the judiciary appears to be relatively honest), while the key corruption issues in Libya center on procurement and in Syria on trade.

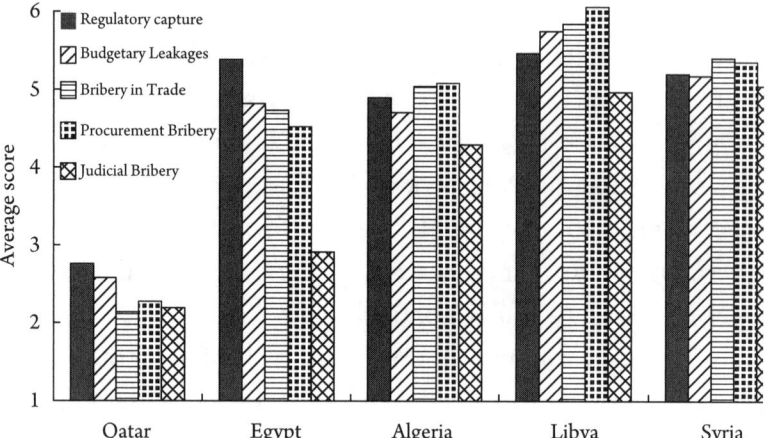

Figure 2.5. Extent of Corruption and Capture in Four Selected Countries. From the results of a survey of firms on the frequency of various types of corruption. (*Source:* World Economic Forum. *Executive Opinion Surveys.* New York: World Economic Forum, 2010.)

More generally, countries in the failing governance group—such as Libya, Syria, Iraq, and Yemen—are already mired in internal conflict, and thus the hoped-for scenario is that they will soon enter the group of postconflict countries and embark on the difficult path toward democratic transition. This group is distinct from the already transitioning countries, such as Egypt and Tunisia, both of which experienced sudden regime change, largely avoiding protracted internal conflict. For Egypt and Tunisia, appropriate strategies would not come from lessons learned from postconflict experiences but from transitions away from autocratic regimes, such as those of central and eastern Europe, the former Soviet Union, Indonesia, Brazil, South Africa, Chile, Turkey, and Spain (see Box 2.1, on some transition lessons).

Other regimes in the region, which currently are neither mired in conflict nor in major transition, may continue to thwart a meaningful transition to democratic governance—some by offering incremental reforms (Jordan, Morocco), some by combining

Box 2.1 SOME LESSONS FROM PREVIOUS TRANSITIONS

It is worth briefly noting five points of relevance from previous transition experiences:

1. Belonging to the select group of Arab Spring countries does not automatically guarantee success. Countries in transitions can traverse into the wrong path (such as Iran and Pakistan), muddle through without meaningful reform for decades (some countries in central Asia), evolve into "managed quasi-democracies" (Russia) or transit into the right direction in democratic governance (Chile, Turkey, Indonesia, and central Europe).

2. Even relatively successful transitions, such as in Indonesia, can take at least a decade until the country is on the right path with setbacks in the early years; thus a patient longer view is needed.*

3. The role and posture of the military are essential, as is the quality of political leadership during the transition (Turkey, Spain, Chile, and South Africa).

4. Effective constitutional and electoral reforms matter, as well as institutional innovations, such as truth and reconciliation commissions (South Africa and Chile).

5. The extent to which the political and economic transitions evolve into an increasingly captured economy (Ukraine) or a competitive enabling environment instead (central Europe) matters enormously.

*In August 2011, Ahmed Heikal, Egypt's largest private investor, said to *The Economist*: "If we get things right, we could be Turkey in ten years. If we get them wrong, we could be Pakistan in 18 months."

payouts from their oil wealth to their relatively small population of nationals (Saudi Arabia and some Gulf countries), and some with further repression (Iran, Bahrain).

MYTHS AND REALITIES IN TRANSITION

The reason for the Arab Spring was the economic discontent of youth, the group that was most seriously excluded from the old welfare state, suffered the most from unemployment, and felt the greatest impact of poor public services and a failing education system. But this perspective must be nuanced. Opinion polls suggest that youth in the Arab world in 2010 (respondents aged 15 to 24) were actually more positive about the economic situation and more optimistic about the future than older respondents. Citizens in the Arab world were actually happier with their lives than the average for the rest of the world and only marginally less happy in those Arab countries embracing the reform movement than in those that are not. So reported unhappiness does not seem to have been a major trigger for the Arab Spring, at least as measured by the now standard "best possible life" question, introduced by Howard Cantril decades ago: ""[I]magine a ladder with steps numbered 0–10. Suppose 10 represents the best possible life for you, and 0 represents the worst possible life for you. On which step of the ladder would you say you personally feel you stand?"

The discontent seems to be more closely related to a growing disillusionment with economic prospects. Expected happiness in the future is lower in the Arab Spring countries than in the rest of the world. In a multivariate analysis across countries, living in one of the Arab Spring countries was significantly associated with lower expectations for future happiness in 2010.[15] Other important predictors of future happiness: a good job market, living in a big city, and having a higher household income, all factors with low scores in Arab Spring countries.

The negative perceptions about the future are what drive the apparent paradox of "unhappy growth" in Arab Spring countries. The paradox is that, while macroeconomic indicators of welfare, such as GDP per capita, were rising in the last few years at reasonably rapid rates, people living in the countries did not feel better off. Opinion polls showed that the share of those describing themselves as thriving (a combination of their current and future expectations of economic well-being) fell from 24 percent to 10 percent of the population in Tunisia between 2008 and 2010 and from 25 percent to 12 percent in Egypt between 2007 and 2010. This happened despite steady growth in per capita GDP (Figure 2.6).

Almost all Arab countries have seen a decline in the share of the population describing themselves as thriving (Figure 2.7), and, as borne out by econometric analysis, there appears to be an association between low levels of popular satisfaction, as measured by this index, and pressures to reform. Egypt, Tunisia, Libya, Morocco, Syria, and Yemen all show low and declining levels of satisfaction. Algeria and Lebanon have so far been spared significant unrest but have higher levels of satisfaction, and more Palestinians seem to be thriving than before. Rich Arab countries still enjoy high levels of life satisfaction.

One reason why people's happiness may have declined was because of the collapse in satisfaction with public services. In just one year, between 2009 and 2010, satisfaction with public transportation systems in Egypt fell by 30 percentage points; satisfaction

15 Chattopadhyay and Graham (2011) using Gallup World Poll survey data.

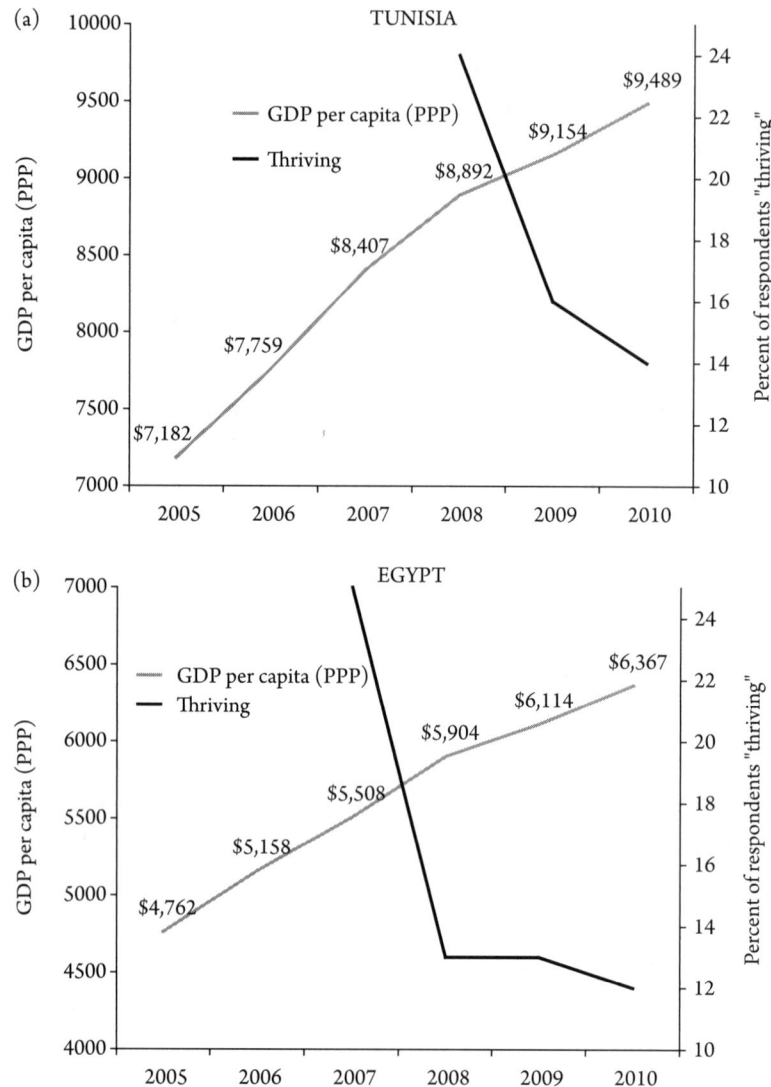

Figure 2.6. Trends in Official Gross Domestic Product per Capita versus Well-Being. Percentage of citizens who report "thriving" in Gallup polls. (*Sources:* John Clifton and Lymari Morales. "Egyptians', Tunisians' Well-Being Plummets Despite GDP Gains." Washington, DC: Gallup Inc., 2011, available at www.gallup.com; 2005–2011 data on GDP per capita from International Monetary Fund. Economic Outlook Database. Washington, DC: IMF, 2011, available at www.imf.org.)

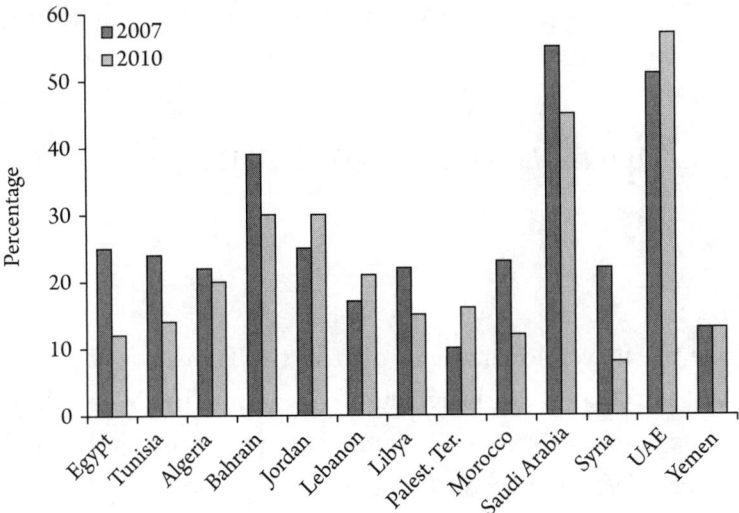

Figure 2.7. Trends in Well-Being. Percentage of citizens who report "thriving" in Gallup polls. For countries that Gallup did not survey in 2007, the earliest available numbers are used. For Tunisia, Algeria, and Syria, 2008 was the first year they were surveyed; 2009 was the first year Bahrain and Libya were surveyed. (*Source:* Data from Gallup World Poll survey.)

with efforts to support the environment fell by 15 percentage points and with housing by 14 percentage points.[16] The latter two issues show both a large deterioration and a low level of satisfaction. Housing and health care show similarly large declines in Tunisia. Even in the case of schools and education, which had been seen by international organizations as a relative success in the Arab world,[17] reported citizen satisfaction had started to decline. These data suggest that overall satisfaction with government delivery of services had started to decline swiftly.

16 Gallup Report, (2010), "Egypt: The Arithmetic of Revolution" (Abu Dhabi: Gallup Center).

17 United Nations Development Programme, (2010), "Arab Human Development Report" (New York: UNDP).

Chapter 3

Opportunities for Young People

While the act of Mohammed Bouazizi, the Tunisian street vendor, served as a catalyst for the revolution, it is youth like Wael Ghonim, the Google executive, who are symbols of the political and economic transition. Wael represents the success that most young Egyptians, and every Arab youth, dream of obtaining. He has a decent job, he is married, and he is upwardly mobile.

But millions of Arab youth cannot become Wael overnight. Support for an economic reform agenda will depend on whether younger workers—those entering the labor market, those currently unemployed, and those employed in the low-wage informal sector—believe that they will benefit from the transition.

For the foreseeable future, Arab transition economies will have to provide jobs for a large youth population that meet the rising tide of expectations. In the largest Arab economy, Egypt, more than 850,000 youth will enter the workforce every year. The working-age population in the Arab world will continue to rise over the next two decades at faster rates than elsewhere, because of both high population growth and a rising share of the working age population as the "youth bulge" enters the labor force.

In large part, public support for the transition will hinge on whether greater opportunities follow new freedoms for the young generation. In particular, this means improvements in young people's employment prospects. This chapter presents an overview of the major challenges facing young people, how they might fare in the transition, and outlines a framework for how transition countries can achieve greater intergenerational equity.

BASIC DEMOGRAPHIC TRENDS

The region's current population is more than 340 million, having grown by 2.6 percent annually from an estimated 81 million in 1950. Population growth is now slowing as fertility rates have declined since 1980, to a level of 2.8 children per woman, about the same as in South Asia. Yet the decline in fertility in the Arab world happened later than in other middle-income regions, and that caused a spike in the numbers of young people.

The Arab population today is dominated by the young. Nearly 55 percent of the population is under the age of 24 and two-thirds are under 30. A region with relatively heavy child dependency in 1970, when those aged 0 to 14 made up as much as 45 percent of the region's population, now faces large numbers of young people joining the workforce. This has led to two seemingly contrarian trends. The Arab world has had the fastest growth of employment between 1998 and 2008 of any region in the world (3.3 percent annually) but still has the second-highest level of unemployment in the world (9.7 percent). It also has a low labor force participation rate of only 50.9 percent (only sub-Saharan Africa has a lower rate), largely because the female labor force participation rate, at 25 percent, is by far the lowest ratio in the world.[1] Fewer than 25 percent of Egyptian women report being employed within five years of graduation.[2]

1 International Labour Organization, (2009), "Growth, Employment and Decent Work in the Arab Region: Key Policy Issues," Thematic Paper (Beirut: ILO)..

2 Ragui Assaad and Ghada Barsoum, (2007), *Youth Exclusion in Egypt: In Search of "Second Chances,"* Middle East Youth Initiative Working Paper (2) (Washington, DC: Brookings Institution, Wolfensohn Center for Development).

There are many more young Arabs (aged 15 to 24) today—about 20 percent of the region's population—compared to Europe, North America, and Latin America where the share is 15 percent or less. The youth share has been rising slowly over the last 30 years and has now peaked.

EMPLOYMENT: YOUNG AND WAITING

Finding a job has been especially difficult for these young workers, who suffer from unemployment rates that are two to three times higher than the average (Figure 3.1), and for women. Algeria, Jordan, and Saudi Arabia have the highest youth unemployment rates, and even Egypt's youth unemployment is currently about 25 percent.

The problem is compounded by the fact that many Arab youth are unprepared to enter the labor force. Only one-quarter has had prior experience of working: the youth employment-to-population ratio stands at 26.8 percent (2008) compared to 53 percent in East Asia. The average unemployment rate for youth was 22 percent in 2008 (again among the highest rates in the world) and 28 percent for young females.

High levels of youth unemployment are linked to the search for a good job in the formal sector. As these employment opportunities became fewer, the duration of the transition from school to work actually fell, with more young people accepting jobs in the informal sector. In Egypt, the time from leaving school to a first job fell to 1.7 years for someone born between 1986 and 1990,[3] but the probability of the first job being in the informal sector rose. In

3 Ragui Assaad, Christine Binzel, and May Galladah, (2010), "Transitions to Employment and Marriage among Young Men in Egypt" (Washington, DC: The Brookings Institution, Wolfensohn Center for Development).

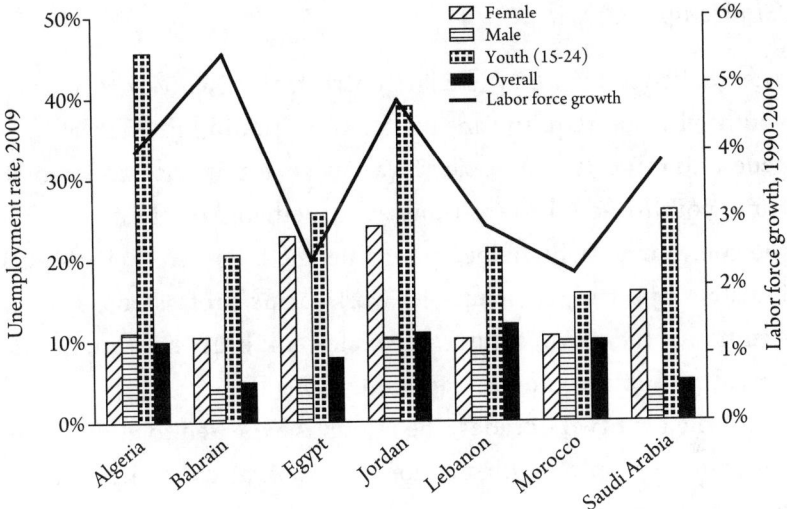

Figure 3.1. Unemployment Rates and Labor Force Growth Rate in Select Arab Countries. *Note:* Latest year available; female, male, and youth unemployment are indicated as a percentage of the female, male, and youth labor force respectively. (*Source:* Jad Chaaban. "Job Creation in the Arab Economies: Navigating Through Difficult Waters." Arab Human Development Report Research Paper Series. New York: United Nations Development Programme, 2010; World Bank. *World Development Indicators,* http://data.worldbankorg/indicator; International Labour Organization. "Key Indicators of the Labour Market." Geneva: ILO, 2011.)

the mid-1970s, 80 percent of first-time job seekers found employment in a formal wage or salary job; by the mid-2000s, only 30 percent did. Those who managed to get a good public sector job had to wait longer after leaving school—suffering through 2.3 years of unemployment.

The labor market conditions directly affect a second major transition faced by youth, the transition to marriage and the formation of their own household unit. Getting a first job increases the probability of marrying by nearly two times;[4] if the job is in the formal sector, the effect is almost immediate. Returning migrants similarly become more attractive marriage partners. The policy conclusion is that the quality of jobs as well as the availability matters.

4 Op. cit.

Challenges Ahead

The challenge for a new social contract, then, is how to provide youth with the requisite means for transitioning to adulthood. A generation ago, when society was more traditional and mostly rural, youth-to-adult transitions were mediated by the family and the community, who helped young people follow in their parents' footsteps by setting them up with work, farms, professions, and new families of their own.[5] Later, the state took over that function by providing public sector jobs and other benefits.

In the next two decades, the region is expected to add another 150 million people, so job creation in most Arab countries will have to exceed 3 percent a year in order to absorb these young job seekers.[6] In Algeria, Iran, Jordan, and Syria the job replacement ratio—the number of youth entering the labor force (say, 20 to 24 years old) compared to the number of an equal-sized part of the population exiting the labor force (aged 60 to 64)—is five; the ratio was closer to four in Egypt, Lebanon, Morocco, and Yemen. This ratio is less than two in developed countries such as Korea and the United States.

These demographic pressures have strained the capability of Arab countries to provide their large youth populations with quality education and jobs. In countries where the growth of this demographic is peaking and large numbers of youth are of marriageable age, demands for affordable housing and other goods are increasing. At the same time, young Arabs lack social networks and the support structure to find a job—labor market information and job placement services are lacking, and informal word-of-mouth approaches

---

5 Alan Richards and John Waterbury, (2008), *A Political Economy of the Middle East* (Boulder, CO: Westview Press).

6 Marcus Noland and Howard Pack, (2007), *The Arab Economies in a Changing World* (Washington, DC: Peterson Institute for International Economics).

through friends and family are the only options for the young. Those structures cannot readily handle the significant numbers of youth now entering the labor market.

Youth expectations have failed to keep up with the reality that the public sector can no longer provide them with jobs. Public sector wages and benefits remain high, propped up by oil wealth or fiscal deficits. Young people are unprepared to take private sector or informal jobs, even if these jobs enhance their skills, unless they are desperate for work. In some households, remittances or public subsidies raise household incomes enough to allow young people the luxury of waiting for the right public sector job to come along.[7] Societal norms encourage parents to support their children well into their twenties rather than having them accept low-status employment.

The incentives to prolong job searches reduce self-reliance early in life and distort how young people respond to labor market reforms. In Jordan, when the government introduced programs to significantly increase job creation, the openings were filled with foreign workers as young Jordanians preferred to wait for better jobs,[8] entering what has been called "waithood": a stretch of time that a large proportion of Arab youth spend waiting to marry, move out of their parent's house, and become full-fledged adults.[9]

7 John Blomquist, (2008), "Are Reservation Wages of the Young 'Too High?'—Evidence from Egypt." Paper presented at the Third IZA/World Bank Conference on Employment and Development, May 5–6, in Rabat, Morocco; Masood Karshenas, (2001), "Economic Liberalization, Competitiveness and Women's Employment in the Middle East and North Africa," in Djavad Salehi-Isfahani, ed., *Labor and Human Capital in the Middle East: Studies of Labor Markets and Household Behavior* (Reading, UK: Ithaca Press).

8 Taher Kanaan and May Hanania, (2009), "Youth Exclusions in Jordan," in N. Dhillon and T. Yousef, eds., *A Generation in Waiting* (Washington, DC: Brookings Institution Press); Susan Razzaz and Farrukh Iqbal, (2008), "Job Growth Without Unemployment Reduction: The Experience of Jordan" (Washington, DC: World Bank).

9 Navtej Dhillon and Tarek Yousef, (2009), *Generation in Waiting: The Unfulfilled Promise of Young People in the Middle East* (Washington, DC: Brookings Institution Press).

EDUCATION—RIGHT INTENTIONS, WRONG OUTCOMES

One of the most vexing problems facing Arab societies is that even educated youth suffer from very high rates of unemployment. Students in the region work hard and pass countless tests to get into a university, only to find themselves unable to find a job, get married, and move out of their parents' home.[10] Moreover, available evidence suggests the economic returns to basic schooling—the extra wages and salaries that can be earned given the number of years spent in school—in Arab countries are particularly low.[11]

The problem with education is not the usual one of a shortage of resources. In the past 40 years, public spending on education in the Arab world, both as a percentage of GDP and per pupil, has been higher than in a sample of comparable East Asian and Latin American countries.[12] Yet the results of these expenditures in terms of quality of education have been disappointing as evidenced by high graduate unemployment rates and low rankings in international educational achievement tests. In 2007, the 14 Arab countries that participated in the Trends in International Mathematics and Science Studies (TIMSS) all scored well below the average (500) and mostly below the "intermediate benchmark" (475), except for Bahraini and Jordanian girls in science. Arab countries took 14 of the bottom 21 positions in the list of 54 countries (see Figure 3.2).

10 Navtej Dhillon and Tarek Yousef, (2009), *Generation in Waiting: The Unfulfilled Promise of Young People in the Middle East* (Washington, DC: Brookings Institution Press).

11 Lant Pritchett, (1999), "Has Education Had a Growth Payoff in the MENA Region?" Middle East and North Africa Working Paper 18 (Washington, DC: World Bank); S. Makdisi, Z. Fattah, and I. Limam, (2006), "Determinants of Growth in the MENA Region," in J. Nugent and M. H. Pesaran, eds., *Explaining Growth in Middle East and North Africa*, (London: Elsevier).

12 World Bank, (2008), *The Road Not Traveled: Education Reform in the Middle East and North Africa* (Washington, DC: World Bank), p. 11.

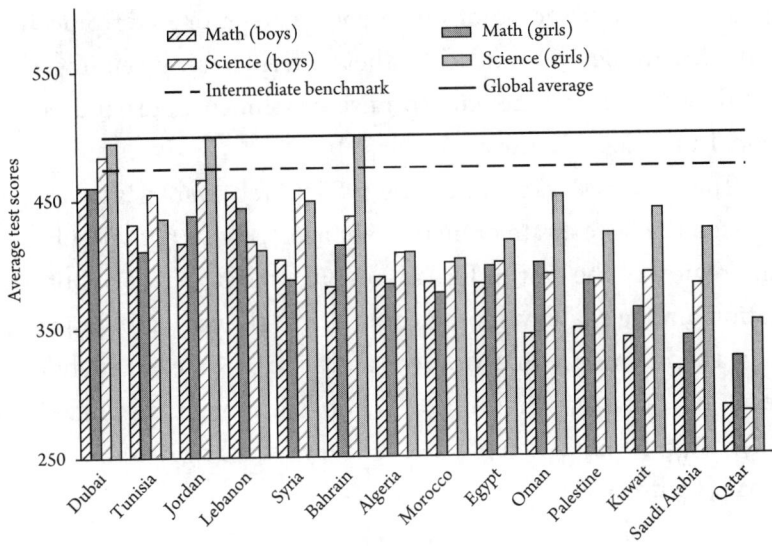

Figure 3.2. Average TIMSS Scores on Grade 8 Mathematics and Science Test, Arab Countries, 2007. (*Source:* Djavad Salehi-Isfahani, Nadia Belhaj Hassine, and Ragui Assaad (2011). "Equality of Opportunity in Education in the Middle East and North Africa." Working paper (Cairo: Economic Research Forum)).

Deep structural reasons exist for the low productivity of education in the Arab world, having to do with the policy environment and the institutions that govern employment and the production of human capital.

Education Policies and Their Success

Historically, formal schooling was a means by which governments trained manpower for the civil service as part of modernizing their administrations. In the latter part of the twentieth century, after independence, a push for formal schooling and education for all became the instrument of choice for Arab nationalist governments to modernize their societies and foster economic development. To encourage formal schooling, they expanded access to free public schools and opened their rapidly growing bureaucracies to their graduates. Governments in Egypt and Morocco went so far as to guarantee public sector jobs to anyone who graduated from a high school. Families responded to these incentives by sending their children to schools, helping to raise enrollment rates and educational attainment in the region.

The policies worked. Since the 1980s, Arab countries have experienced the fastest rate of increase in average years of schooling in any region of the world. Jordan now has the highest level of education among the developing countries in the region, followed by Libya and Tunisia, while Morocco and Syria provide relatively lower levels of education (Figure 3.3). School enrollment rates have been likewise quite high, except for secondary schooling in Morocco and Syria (Figure 3.4).

Falling Skills, Rising Credentialism

Over time, however, the limitations of this system of expanding the supply side of education have become clear. In the process, a "credentialist equilibrium" was formed in which the government, the main employer of the educated, focused on hiring those students getting diplomas and degrees from the best schools and universities. Universities, in turn, taught curricula that allowed for quantitative testing, grading, and the sorting and ranking of students, who strived to get into the best schools. The system was in equilibrium because the government was able to recruit students demonstrating knowledge, ability, and diligence; schools achieved high graduation rates; and students competed for their preferred jobs in the public sector.

The search for credentials, coupled with the increasing size of the student-age population, has ratcheted up the level of education that a graduate must have in order to be eligible for a government job. Flushed with abundant applicants, governments have raised their minimum standards for employment, in most cases now requiring a minimum of a university degree.

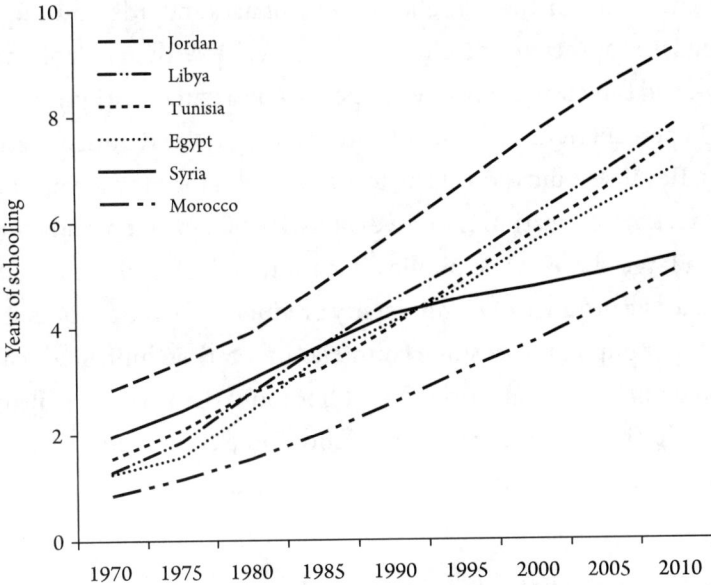

Figure 3.3 Average Years of Schooling for Selected Arab Countries, Working-age Population, 15–59 Years. (*Source:* Robert J. Barro and Jong-Wha Lee (2010). "A New Data Set of Educational Attainment in the World, 1950-2010." NBER working paper 15902 (Cambridge, MA: NBER)).

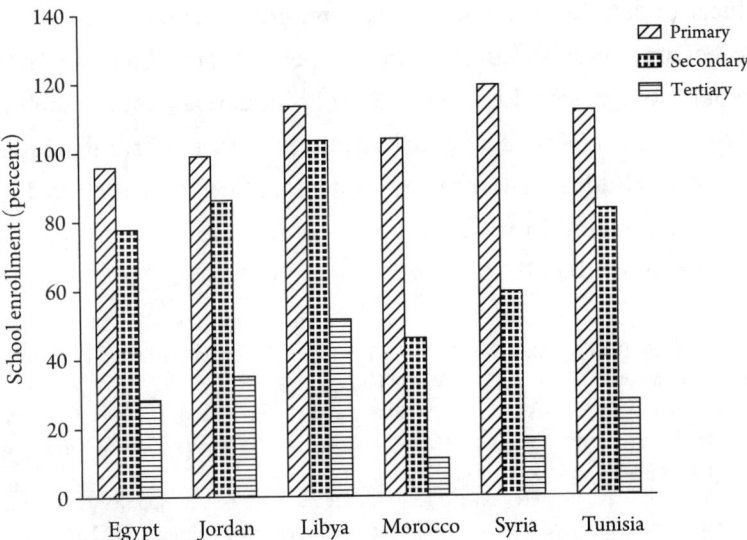

Figure 3.4 School Enrollment Rates in Selected Arab Countries (percent). 2000s decade average. (*Source:* World Bank. *World Development Indicators,* http://data.world-bankorg/indicator, 2008.

The result of these higher educational standards and requirements is a top-heavy enrollment structure. More than half of university-aged Libyans are enrolled in postsecondary education, followed by 35 percent in Jordan and 28 percent in Egypt and Tunisia (Figure 3.4). Because education at the tertiary level is for the most part free, and tertiary education is more expensive than primary and secondary, a large share of the public education budget in these countries goes to the production of university graduates.[13] Arab schools spend more per pupil (and in some countries in total) on higher education than on primary education. Egypt has more than twice the proportion of university graduates in its labor force compared to Turkey, a country with three times the per capita income.[14]

The Credentialist Bargain Distorts Education Expenditures, Quality, and Equity

The influence of university education on schools is not limited to the draining of public education resources. As demand for university education has outstripped supply, competition to enter universities has become fierce, forcing families to spend greater resources on test preparation, which adds little by way of productive human capital. In 1994, in Egypt 64 percent of urban and 51 percent of rural primary-schoolage children had received supplementary tutoring.[15] In 1997, household expenditures on supplementary tutoring accounted for 1.6 percent of the GDP,[16] more than a quarter of all public expen-

13 World Bank, (2008), *The Road Not Traveled: Education Reform in the Middle East and North Africa* (Washington, DC: World Bank), p. 123.

14 Djavad Salehi-Isfahani, Insaf Tulani, and Ragui Assaad, (2009), "A comparative study of returns to education of urban men in Egypt, Iran and Turkey," *Middle East Development Journal* 1(2): 145–187.

15 Mark Bray and Percy Kwok, (2003), "Demand for private supplementary tutoring: conceptual considerations, and socio-economic patterns in Hong Kong," *Economics of Education Review* 22: 611–620.

16 World Bank, (2002), *Arab Republic of Egypt: Education Sector Review-Progress and Priorities in the Future* (Washington, DC: World Bank), p. 26.

ditures on education. The race to pass the tests required to enter a university dominates education below the university level and is a distinct feature of the "credentialist equilibrium" today.

Rising enrollments and limited resources for education at the primary and secondary levels forced schools to enlarge class sizes and use multiple-choice tests as a way to motivate students. The alternative motivation—interest in the subject matter—requires keeping class sizes small and teachers well paid, which are luxuries that only select private schools could afford. As a result, public education systems in Arab countries have morphed into giant diploma mills that reward rote learning and investment in a narrow range of skills that lend themselves to multiple-choice testing.[17] Creative skills, such as writing and problem solving, which are costly to acquire but do not add much to the probability of entering a university, receive little attention from teachers and parents.

Not surprisingly, the returns to schooling at primary and lower secondary levels are nearly zero, while they are relatively high at the university level.[18] Most of the students enrolled at the secondary level who will not get into university would do well to drop out of the race and learn other skills instead. A strategy of tracking students at grade nine (about age 15) is in effect in many countries to prevent low achievers from staying in the race for too long. These students then get sent to technical and vocational schools to learn some practical skills.[19]

Increasing scarcity of public sector jobs has not fundamentally redirected students' outlook and prospects away from the public sector. The public sector is still the primary employer of university-educated workers, helping to keep hopes high for those still in

---

17 World Bank, (2008), *The Road Not Traveled: Education Reform in the Middle East and North Africa* (Washington, DC: World Bank), p. 49.

18 Djavad Salehi-Isfahani, Insaf Tulani, and Ragui Assaad, (2009), "A comparative study of returns to education of urban men in Egypt, Iran and Turkey," *Middle East Development Journal* 1 (2): 145-187.

19 World Bank, (2008), *The Road Not Traveled*, p. 146.

school. In Egypt and Tunisia, young educated workers apply for public sector jobs that can take years to materialize. This is especially true for young women. In Tunisia the position of a young person in these applicant pools and on waiting lists is considered an important signal of his future prospects. In Syria, a study of youth attitudes found that more than 80 percent of unemployed 15- to 29-year-olds preferred jobs in the public sector, and 60 percent sought jobs exclusively in the public sector.

While it is commonplace to describe the phenomenon of high unemployment rates of the educated Arab youth as a mismatch of skills, this description is only partially correct. In reality, there is a good match between what students learn in the region's schools and what they perceive their future employers in the public sector need—a diploma. Although the role of public sector employment has waned in recent years across the region, an unhappy equilibrium persists with students still coveting public sector jobs and the higher education system still sorting students into a hierarchical list in a way that makes it easier for the public sector to choose the best and the brightest. The public sector is still the primary employer of the university-educated labor force, and a good university degree is the main prerequisite for being hired by the civil service or a state-owned enterprise. Thus, the degree qualification, not the skills learned, remains the key to future success. That must change (Box 3.1).

In this regard, the Arab higher education system has failed to impart the skills and knowledge needed for the twenty-first century workplace, despite large investments in universities. Arab countries have expanded higher education quantity but not quality: Of the top 500 universities around the world, depending on the system of ranking used, only between zero and six are in Arab countries. When ranked against other countries on a per-capita basis, the output of scientific and technical journal publications from Arab countries is far below what would be expected based on GDP and is among the lowest in the world (see Figure 3.5).

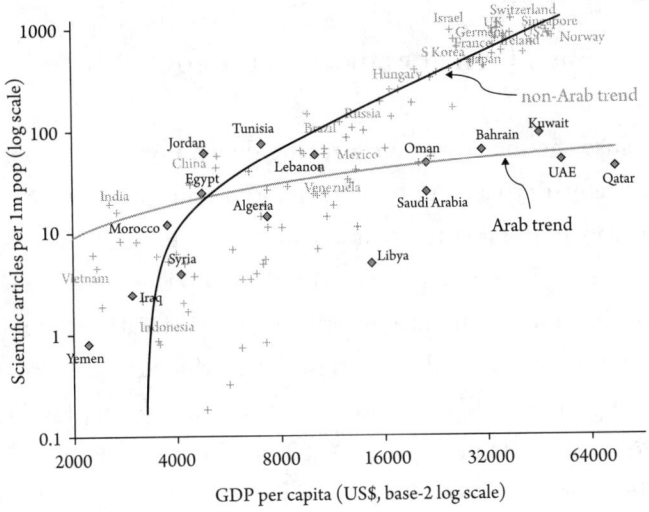

Figure 3.5 Scientific Output by Income Level in Comparative Perspective, 2007. (*Source:* World Bank. *World Development Indicators*, http://data.worldbankorg/indicator, 2008.)

Significantly, the race to get into a university has only increased the inequality of opportunity in education, which the initial support for education by the postcolonial government had aimed to eliminate. This is because with tighter competition for the limited spots in top schools, families spend enormous resources on private schools and private tutoring. With the expanded influence of private resources in determining a child's life chances, inequality of opportunity in education has reached levels usually observed only in Latin America. The share of inequality in educational achievement (test scores in science and mathematics on the TIMSS test) that is explained by family background and community characteristics is estimated at about one-third in Dubai, Egypt, Jordan, Lebanon, Qatar, Saudi Arabia, and Tunisia and one-fourth in the rest. Only Algeria and Morocco have relatively low inequality of opportunity.[20]

20 Djavad Salehi-Isfahani, Nadia Belhaj Hassine, and Ragui Assad, (2011), "Equality of Opportunity in Education in the Middle East and North Africa," *Economic Research Forum*, http://www.econ.vt.edu/seminars/seminarpapers/2011/salehi09162011.pdf.

Box 3.1 THE CREDENTIALIST EQULIBRIUM

Because the incentives for learning depend on wage differentials, reforms that focus on schools alone and ignore distortions in the incentives structure in the larger economy are less likely to succeed. This was the case with the region's experience with technical and vocational education (TVE) in its attempt to shift priorities toward skill formation. The evidence for increased earnings from TVE education is mixed. The evidence for Egypt is that the gains in wages and salaries from completing TVE were lower than those for general secondary education largely because of high attrition.* One reason for the lackluster performance of the region's TVE is the way students are selected through written tests for training in trades. Students pursuing TVE were barred from the academic track and bear the stigma of low ability, so many who enroll in it see it as punishment for failing rather than as way to acquire productive skills. Many graduates of the program face the prospect of working solely in the informal sector, so they prefer to drop out. To keep attrition at TVE schools low, some countries offer paths for TVE graduates to continue on to university, reinforcing the "credentialist equilibrium." However, this pattern is not universal; in Lebanon, returns to TVE actually exceed those for general secondary education, indicating that, despite the adverse selection, those who eschew the university route may do better.‡

*Djavad Salehi-Isfahani, (2009), "Education and Earnings in the Middle East: A Comparative Study of Returns to Schooling in Egypt, Iran and Turkey," Economic Research Forum Working Paper 504, available at http://www.erf.org.eg/CMS/uploads/pdf/504.pdf.
‡World Bank MENA Development Report, (2007), *The Road Not Traveled: Education Reform in the Middle East and North Africa* (Washington, DC: World Bank).

continued from previous page

The signals from the private sector for the type of skills it is willing to reward remain weak, and it is not easy for private employers to provide market-based signals for the skills they need. Wages are distorted by considerable regulations in the labor market. As a result, the education system has shown considerable inertia and has found it easier to churn out diplomas than teach twenty-first-century skills. As the number of youth going through the school system got larger, the tendency to only teach skills that lend themselves to large-scale testing has increased, and the ability to promote productive skills that do not lend themselves to multiple-choice testing, such as writing, teamwork, and innovative research, areas where greater teacher resources are required, has declined.

Even where the private sector is stronger, as in Egypt, Jordan, and Tunisia, the status of private employment remains low and has not improved despite reforms since the 1990s. This holds for Jordan and Tunisia, where a significant part of job creation was in private, formal employment as well as for Egypt where most private employment was informal.· It does not seem likely that student attitudes will change in the aftermath of the Arab Spring. The national mood may turn even further against private sector jobs before it turns in their favor.

These reflections suggest that a major overhaul of the education system is needed, involving changing students' expectations, altering curricula (including the private sector to understand the need for skills in a modern economy), and

· Mohamed Hassan and Cyrus Sassanpour, (2008), "Labor Market Pressures in Egypt: Why Is the Unemployment Rate so Stubbornly High?" presented at the International Conference on "The Unemployment Crisis in the Arab World," http://www.arab-api.org/conf_0308/p7.pdf.

continued from previous page

changing civil service requirements. All these changes need to take place in a coherent, long-term, comprehensive endeavor, or else the system will revert back to its current equilibrium. Multiple stakeholders, including businesses, government administrators, educators, families, and youth groups, have to be brought together to develop a long-range program for change. Otherwise the credentialist equilibrium will become too entrenched.

TRANSITION CHALLENGE: EVENING OUT THE BURDEN OF ADJUSTMENT

Successful youth-to-adult transitions require young people to gain the right skills while in school, engage in a purposeful search for a job or career, avoid risky behavior, and, in good time, start families. This has not been happening, and young people have borne a disproportionate share of the costs of adjustment and slow reforms over the past three decades, from the state-led model of development that characterized the postcolonial era to more market-oriented development strategies.

As evident from previous transitions in other regions, the costs of transition will not fall evenly on all age groups.[21] Younger people have high expectations that the transition will improve their lives. However, the risk is that policies enacted during the transition will rely on existing institutions that have had longstanding biases against young people.

21 See Richard Freeman, (1992), "What Direction for Labor Market Institutions? Transition in Eastern Europe," NBER Working Paper 4209 (Cambridge, MA: NBER).

Ensure Policies Do Not Just Reward Incumbents

Examples of policy decisions and actions that shift the adjustment burden onto young people abound. The most notable is how in the past public sector employment was curtailed by simply freezing or dramatically slowing new hiring and relying mostly on attrition to achieve workforce reductions. To date, there have not been large-scale layoffs of public sector employees anywhere in the region, and only minimal downsizing was achieved through voluntary early retirement schemes. On the other hand, there was a large decline in the share of educated graduates that were able to obtain public sector jobs and an increase in graduate unemployment. The small size of the formal private sector, combined with its fairly slow employment growth, meant that a growing proportion of new entrants from the youth bulge generation were relegated to low-quality jobs in the informal economy.

Public sector employment reforms were typically accompanied by selective labor law reforms that provided private sector employers with greater flexibility in hiring and firing and by reduced enforcement of labor laws. Reformed regulations made it easier for employers to use definite duration contracts and allowed them to end indefinite duration contracts in case of economic necessity with or without the payment of severance. Again, these reforms were introduced in such a way as to grandfather any workers with existing contracts under the old rules and apply the new, more flexible rules to new hires only. Admittedly, these more flexible employment regulations may have made it more likely for new entrants to be hired formally rather than off the books,[22] but they

22 Jackline Wahba, (2009), "The Impact of Labor Market Reforms on Informality in Egypt," Gender and Work in the MENA Region Working Paper Series, Number 3. (New York: The Population Council).

also concentrated the impact of any employment adjustments on young new entrants, making them more vulnerable to economic downturns.

Housing offers a similar example of the burden of adjustment being forced disproportionately onto youth. With appreciating real exchange rates, there has been a boom in housing prices in many Arab economies. Those who already had access to public housing and subsidy schemes benefited hugely from this boom, but as public programs were cut back, newcomers into the housing market, mostly young people, were essentially shut out by high market prices. Surveys suggest a dramatic increase in the dissatisfaction with public services in the housing sector in recent years.

Going forward, the policy and institutional bias against young people must be reversed without reviving the unsustainable and inefficient approaches of the old social contract. That is not easy to accomplish. In most reforms, it is politically simpler to act on the margin, but in cases where stronger reforms are needed, as in many Arab economies, it may be necessary to go beyond marginal changes where incumbents are always grandfathered. All of society has to be brought together to share the burden of the transition in an equitable fashion, or else the aspirations of today's youth will once more be dashed.

Government cutbacks in hiring cannot, and should not, be reversed to accommodate young people. The public sector has an important role to play in changing expectations and job preferences of the young, and reforms should be consistent with long-term policies, to the extent possible. What should be avoided are short-term policies that distort labor market signals. That is why the decision of Egypt's transitional government to expand public employment and convert workers from temporary contract employees to permanent civil servants is a risky approach. It may appease short-term social pressure but risks reinforcing existing attitudes toward the public sector as an employer of first and last resort.

Secure Early Gains for Young People in the Transition

Several steps can be taken to achieve this through policies that create new incentives and signals and lay a foundation for future reforms. A key priority must be to change the "winning group," for too long defined through access to higher education and through public sector employment. Interim and future governments in the course of the transition should use policies to signal a shift in focus that places greater value on civil society organizations, private sector employment, and the role of young people in policy dialogue.

First, in the short term, transition countries should bolster support and open more space for civil society organizations. They play an important role in advancing key economic reforms through advocacy, promoting accountability, and being involved in service delivery. Greater freedom of association and improving NGO registration laws can help create a more supportive environment for young people to contribute to their community. Investing and scaling up in volunteer programs can provide a bridge for school-to-work transitions. For this reason, successful programs such as Teach for America are being introduced elsewhere, including in India and Chile. At a time when social pressures are high in Egypt and Tunisia, expanding the civil society sector can provide critical economic and social benefits as well as generate positive impetus for the transition.

Second, youth employment should be an urgent priority especially as Egypt, Tunisia, and Libya experience a slowdown in growth, a drop in investment, and protracted political processes. Youth employment is one of the most highly sensitive variables in the labor market, falling significantly more during downturns.

In Egypt and Tunisia, there are several government-funded active labor market programs. But they are constrained as they reach a limited number of young beneficiaries, mostly young urban males with a postsecondary education, and there is little evidence of their effectiveness. However, in other countries, direct employment schemes have had a broad impact: Chile Joven and Argentina's Proyecto Joven each provided free, six-month, semiskilled training to 100,000 young people over four years.

Within the region, there are new models of job training and matching under way, such as the National Organization for Women (NOW) project in Jordan that uses vouchers to increase employment for young women. Such programs could be expanded and replicated. Governments can target young workers in key sectors that are vulnerable as growth decelerates (e.g., tourism, construction) with programs that offer cash for work—providing temporary income opportunities to those youth most susceptible to the crisis or through tax incentives to firms to retain young workers. In areas where the interim government is pursuing new investments for skills development, like Egypt's new training centers linked to industrial clusters, learning from other countries could be useful. For example, Malaysia's Penang Skills Development Center is a model for creating an effective skills training program to meet industry needs, with the strong involvement of the private sector.

Finally, assistance and capacity building should be targeted to increase the voice and representation of young people in the development of national and local policy. Starting in 1983, Spain embarked on a process to initiate dialogue with youth associations and organizations that led to the legal establishment of a Council for Spanish Youth. In former central and eastern European countries, the development of national and local youth councils was effective in increasing young people's participation in political and economic transition and reforms. Similarly today, in Egypt and Tunisia, there are emerging efforts toward organizing youth groups through national and local youth bodies. These efforts can be supported and accelerated through assistance that provides capacity building, training, and lessons from other transition economies.

Medium-Term Reforms Necessary for Youth Inclusion

In the medium term, comprehensive reforms in education and the labor market are vital for reorienting the economy to be more inclusive. There needs to be a shift of incentives from the accumulation of diplomas and degrees that have value in a shrinking public sector to human capital that is valued by the private sector. This requires deep institutional changes involving labor markets (for example, linking pay and job security to productivity) and social insurance (unemployment and health insurance).

To encourage schools and families in Arab countries to move away from the production of diplomas to the production of human capital, the perceived returns to the latter must increase, and the only way to do so is for the private sector to have a greater role in shaping perceptions of what will get rewarded in the labor market. This will not happen as long as the private sector resorts to informality in its hiring practices. Informal jobs are considered much inferior compared to government jobs, and will be shunned by students in favor of continued attempts at securing jobs in government. Hence, governments should prioritize reforms that make it easier for small and new firms, where most private sector jobs originate, to register and become formal.

Despite the fact that the dominance of the public sector in the labor market will be phased out over time, given the political difficulties, policy makers can still use public employment to generate new signals for human capital development. Hiring for all government employment programs should be linked to an individual's productivity and skills, for example language and writing skills as opposed to formal certificates.

Countries such as Tunisia and Egypt are entering the economic transition with some of the highest literacy rates among previous transition countries. The value of education among parents and youth is extremely high. Thus support for broad reforms can be created by focusing on making education systems more accountable to parents and students; reevaluating and better targeting of free education at the tertiary level; reforming curriculum, standards, and teacher incentives; creating new regulatory frameworks for the private sector to play a better and bigger role in the provision of higher education; and introducing new elements into national entrance examinations to provide incentives for younger generations to broaden skills such as writing and problem solving.

Education, labor markets, and even family formation (housing and credit markets) have been the target of government policy for some time. A major lapse, however, has been to treat these as disconnected from one another. Instead, thinking of these issues in terms of their effects on youth inclusion would lead to more attention being given to the incentives faced by young people and the domestic institutions that generate these incentives. Without change in both of these areas and a better appreciation for the life courses and transitions of young people, effective policy change cannot be developed (Box 3.2).

Box 3.2 WHAT NEXT FOR A GENERATION IN WAITING?

Long before the uprisings swept Arab countries, a generation of young Arab men and women had been gifted with the power to change the trajectories of their countries. They had the strength of a large youth population, were increasingly more educated, and shared a collective consciousness across borders borne out of common struggles. The lives of Ahmed, Saleh, and Fatima present a snapshot of three individuals experiencing and negotiating critical transitions of education, work, and family in three transition countries.

Ahmed, a 26-year-old Jordanian graduated with a degree in Arabic literature and is aspiring for a job in the public sector. He is the first person in his family, and one of the few in the Bedouin community, to have acquired a university degree. He has waited two years for a government job. Living with his parents, his future plans are on hold until he secures a stable and prestigious job.

Saleh, a 19-year-old in Cairo, was tracked into vocational education after failing to obtain a high score in the university entrance exams. Saleh graduated with a diploma in computer repairs but was unsuccessful in finding a job in the formal private sector. After a yearlong search, he joined his uncle's clothing store where he is responsible for measuring and cutting cloth. A small stipend from his uncle enables Saleh to maintain a social life with friends, and his living costs are subsidized by staying with his parents.

Fatima, a 23-year-old Tunisian, is coming of age in a small town. After spending some years in primary and secondary education, she has been unsuccessful in finding decent work.

continued from previous page

An offer of marriage from within the community presents her family with an opportunity to see their daughter successfully transition to adulthood.

Ahmed, Saleh, and Fatima belong to a generation that has faced uncertainty in attaining the right education, securing a quality job, and deciding on when to get married. Aside from this, they have waited for a larger change: for the old system to vanish and a different set of institutions to emerge that can support a new life course.

What do they want? Better education, jobs, credit, affordable housing, and opportunities abroad. But they also want a chance to shape their own destiny, to control the course of their transition. Basically, to fix the so-called mismatch of skills, families and their children need a mind-set change to spend more resources on learning productive skills that private employers demand and less on rote memorization and passing tests; less on private tutoring and more on writing skills, the arts, and team sports. Universities should not be the only place where the acquisition of skills leads to higher personal incomes. The education system has to be restructured such that those who do not complete high school and tertiary degrees still have useful skills to show for their effort.

The difficulty in the new democratic environment is to find the type of politicians who can articulate the goals for these policies and avoid populist traps. A few ideas are:

- An information campaign to educate the public about skills gaps and job opportunities and entrepreneurship awareness programs in high schools.

continued from previous page

- Relating hiring for all government employment programs to the level of an individual's productivity and skills (for example, language skills in the tourist trade as opposed to formal certificates; writing instead of test-taking skills).

- Introducing new elements into national entrance examinations to provide incentives for younger generations to broaden skills such as writing and problem solving. Testing these skills is labor intensive and expensive and cannot be done through multiple-choice tests, which may be why this is not already being done. The army of the educated unemployed could prove helpful in these situations. With minimal training, they could serve as low-cost examiners.

- Quality assurance programs can be introduced to set standards and monitor school achievement through international benchmarking.

Chapter 4

BUILDING A MODERN STATE

The challenge of economic reform in the Arab world is foremost a challenge of state building. It is the credibility of state institutions in managing a complex, long-term process of change that will shape expectations and determine growth and equity outcomes. In past years, Arab governments have been handicapped by deficiencies in the institutional structures of states that were principally created for redistributive and interventionist purposes, were closely connected to the patronage of a ruling clique, and were unable to adapt to new policy demands and changing economic environments. Arab governments, therefore, need the fiscal and regulatory instruments to manage the difficult process of economic transition under conditions of economic volatility and social vulnerability.

This will require a public financial system that is transparent both in terms of budgetary and nonbudgetary components and that can be scrutinized in order for citizens to hold officials accountable for their actions. No less important, governments need to improve the quality and quantity of data on which effective policymaking depends, building more effective infrastructures for data collection and analysis.

It will also require significant improvements to the bureaucracy, the effectiveness of public service provision, and the fight against corruption. Improving the performance of government could entail significant restructuring and dislocation of existing arrangements, a prospect that will likely be fiercely resisted by current insiders.

That transition will require reformers to create conditions in which coalitions that support socially equitable reforms can organize, engage in collective action, and develop as grassroots movements. These groups can take the lead in changing expectations about the public sector as a primary employer and actively support the private sector as an engine of job creation. This includes strengthening collective bargaining frameworks and extending the benefits of formal employment to a larger share of workers even as labor markets become more flexible.

FISCAL REFORM

On the fiscal front, the situation is worrisome in some countries, especially Egypt and Jordan. To start, both the fiscal deficit and domestic public debt are moderate to large in most Arab economies, with the notable exception of Libya (Figure 4.1). While most of the debt is denominated in national currency, and deficits are largely funded domestically, there are still risks. Reinhart and Rogoff (2009)[1] note the significant risk of default on sovereign debt over long historical periods and emphasize that the more recent period in which most countries have honored debt payments is a historical anomaly rather than the norm. They show that even though episodes of default on external creditors tend to get more attention, the frequency of default on domestic creditors is actually higher than external debt defaults in the postwar period, averaging 21 percent per year. The reason is that with fiat money, the ability to implicitly expropriate residents through inflation has become more expedient. What emerges from their long historical analysis

---

1 Carmen Reinhart and Kenneth Rogoff, (2009), *This Time Is Different: Eight Centuries of Financial Folly* (Princeton, NJ: Princeton University Press).

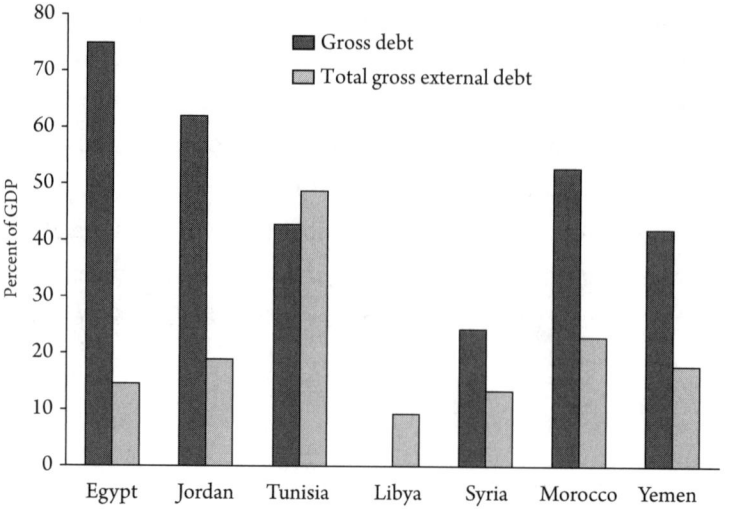

Figure 4.1. Gross Debt and Total Gross External Debt, Percentage of GDP, 2011.
(*Source:* International Monetary Fund. *World Economic Outlook 2011: Middle East and Central Asia.* International Financial Statistics database, 2011.)

is that domestic debt cannot be treated as of less significance than external debt; sometimes residents fare better and sometimes defaults on external creditors come first. Furthermore, they point out that domestic debt crises cannot be dismissed as somehow less problematic than external debt crises. The real GDP loss during an episode of domestic default is significantly worse than the loss due to an external debt crisis. The same is true for the inflationary consequences of sovereign default: the rise in consumer prices in a domestic default episode is far higher than that in an external debt crisis.

Without being alarmist, it is worth looking more closely at fiscal risks in Egypt. Egypt's public debt is high and has a short-term maturity structure with annual rollover needs of 25 percent of the GDP. In response to popular demand, in some cases justifiably so, the government followed expansionary fiscal policy, for example giving compensation to relatives of those killed in the revolution or deferring payment of taxes for two to three months. Some budget actions, however, were not justified and could prove costly in the medium run. The list includes giving permanent contracts to 450,000 temporary employees and premature payment of a 15 percent bonus to civil servants and pensioners. The government's offer to increase new public sector hiring generated seven million applications, showing that the number of disappointed rejected applicants far exceeded the number of happy successful applicants. These measures, along with the announcement that the Egyptian government is working to adjust the wage structure and revise the minimum wage, have again raised expectations that the public sector should be responsible for providing good jobs.

On the revenue side, a similar pattern of appeasing key constituencies in the short term, even if contrary to the long-term direction of policy, has emerged in Egypt. Although the real estate tax only affected a small, relatively wealthy section of the population, the opposition of land owners was enough to block its passage and implementation for a long time. The proposed shift from a general sales tax to a full-fledged value added tax met with a similar fate. At the same time, borrowing costs have gone up as treasury bill yields increased by some 200 basis points from pre-January 25 levels. The fiscal deficit for the year ending June 2011 is now expected to widen by nearly 2 percent of the GDP, reaching 8 to 10 percent of that total. Deficits in Jordan, Syria, and Yemen are also dangerously high (Figure 4.2).

The public deficit figures give a snapshot of what is happening in the short term to debt dynamics, but they cannot be used as a basis for assessing long-term fiscal sustainability. That depends more on the underlying structural deficit that at present is disguised by several factors. First, the exchange rate in many countries is out of equilibrium, supported either by capital controls or by official reserve sales.

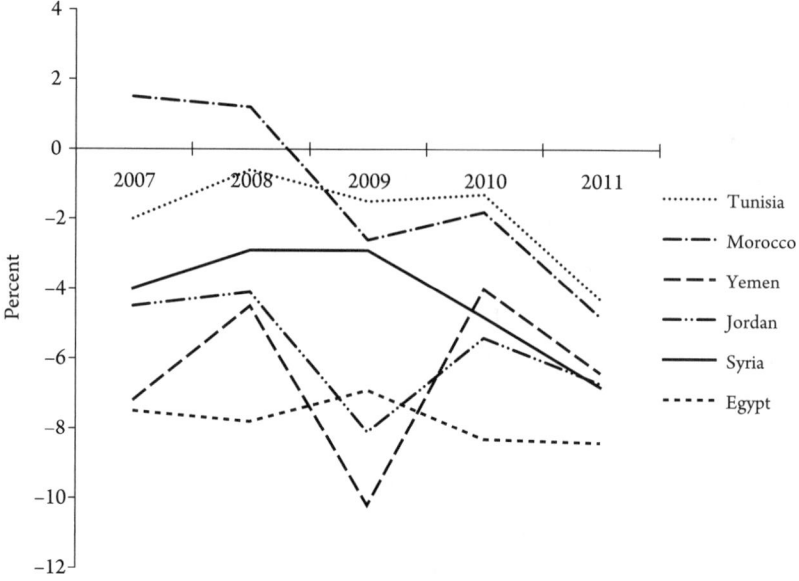

Figure 4.2. Fiscal Balance in Select Arab Countries, Percentage of GDP, 2007–2011. (*Source:* International Monetary Fund. *World Economic Outlook 2011: Middle East and Central Asia.* International Financial Statistics database, 2011.)

Unlike other cases of major economic transition, Arab economies have not witnessed strong currency depreciations as yet. Without more exchange rate adjustments, however, the long-term fundamental reforms to encourage the private sector and increasingly open the economy to the rest of the world will not be successful.

It is hard to predict exactly what the impact of the exchange rate would be on the fiscal deficit. In some cases, where government revenues come from natural resources, a depreciation could reduce the deficit. In other cases, in which subsidies on imported food and fuel are large, a depreciation could increase it. In both cases, the underlying structural deficit should be computed on the basis of an equilibrium exchange rate, not on the basis of the current market rate.

Similarly, structural deficits should account for the economic business cycle. It is reasonable to expect actual deficits to be higher when the economy is in a downturn, as at present, so the structural deficit may be less than the headline deficit. Other factors to be taken into account are the contingent liabilities of state-owned enterprises and banks. In many other countries, banks have suffered during a major economic transition and required assistance from the government, putting additional pressure on government finances.

For all these reasons, it is appropriate for governments to take a cautious attitude toward their fiscal policy in the early stages of a transition. The key task must be to stabilize confidence in long-term debt dynamics, and that requires strong signals and commitments as to how government deficits will evolve and be financed in the future.

The first 18 months after President Hosni Mubarak's resignation are critical for Egypt. Expectations of immediate dividends from the revolution are high at a time when growth has decelerated and unemployment is on the rise. Food and fuel prices are likely to remain at elevated levels and the government's borrowing costs have risen. Nonperforming loans are expected to rise. Meanwhile, the balance of payments has come under increasing pressure as the current account deficit widens and foreign investors wait for elections to take place. According to the government, the financing gap over the next 14 months is estimated at $12 billion ($2 billion for fiscal year (FY) 11 and $10 billion for FY 12). Foreign exchange reserves have been reduced to $19.4 billion at the end of September 2011 from $29.8 billion in February.

The first and most critical step to arrest the deteriorating economic situation is in the hands of the political leadership that urgently needs to give priority to restoring security of individuals and property as well as to putting forward a clear and broadly supported political transition road map. In Egypt, the security situation is unquestionably better than during or immediately after the revolution, but much more needs to be done to face the new sectarian violence and laxity in enforcing the law. Better security and a viable transition plan would help economic agents build confidence in the future, thereby encouraging them to resume production, exports, and domestic and foreign investment. It would also encourage the return of tourists.

Meanwhile, the following suggestions can be made with respect to fiscal policy:

- Resist the tendency to increase the fiscal deficit in response to rising expectations so as to stay consistent with medium-term stability and a sustainable public debt position.
- Seek grants, not loans, to finance public deficits, and use this support as an opportunity to put the macroeconomic situation in order.
- Develop a track record for prudent policies to shape expectations about long-term public debt sustainability.
- Influence change by reconsidering the composition of public expenditures, for example, by expanding programs to benefit the poor and young and to activate the economy through public infrastructure investment, all the while leaving aggregate public spending unchanged.
- Conduct broad-based consultation with stakeholders on the budget, during a transition phase in which democratic representation has yet to take hold.

Dealing with Subsidies

The provision of cheap goods, usually food and energy, is accepted as a key responsibility of Arab governments. For many years, Arab citizens accepted dictatorship, the flaunting of human rights, inefficiency, corruption, and even devastating wars, without calling for regime change. However, when President Anwar Sadat tried to remove bread subsidies in 1977, Egyptians took to the streets, and he had to rescind the decision in order to save his regime.

Food and fuel subsidies are a common feature of Arab economies, but their relative size varies significantly across countries. As a share of GDP, subsidies are highest in Egypt and Yemen, averaging 8 to 9 percent. In Egypt, about 6 percent of the GDP goes to energy subsidies (fuel and electricity), and 2 percent are for food, while nearly the entire subsidy budget in Yemen is for energy products. To put some perspective on those figures, subsidies in Egypt are higher than the entire government wage bill (including for health and education) and are more than double public investment spending. In Libya, subsidies for food, medicines, fuel, electricity, and water are about 6 to 7 percent of the GDP, more or less equal to the wage bill. In Tunisia, subsidies are around 4 percent of the GDP with one-quarter of them for energy products, while in Syria they are 2 to 3 percent of the GDP.[2]

The economic cost of those subsidies goes well beyond the financial cost. At the macroeconomic level, the high degree of subsidies in Egypt and Yemen means that their prospects for growth and poverty reduction continue to be hampered by weak infrastructure and decaying education and health systems. A change in subsidy policies would allow for a reallocation of resources away from consumption and to much needed development and social sector expenditures. The energy subsidies are particularly inefficient, distortionary, and harmful to the environment. The energy and carbon intensity of the Egyptian economy is two and a half to three times higher than the OECD average. Energy subsidies in Egypt are also

2 International Monetary Fund, (2010), *Staff Report for the 2010 Article IV Consultation* (Arab Republic of Egypt: IMF); IMF, (2010), *Staff Report for the 2010 Article IV Consultation* (Tunisia: IMF); IMF, (2010), *Staff Report for the 2009 Article IV Consultation* (Syrian Arab Republic: IMF); and IMF, (2010), *Staff Report for the 2009 Article IV Consultation* (Socialist People's Libyan Arab Jamahiriya: IMF).

highly regressive, as 57 percent of the value is captured by the top two quintiles of the population.[3]

Generalized food subsidies are inconsistent with Arab countries' strategies for food and nutrition security. Arab countries are the largest cereal importers in the world, with Egypt being the world's largest wheat importer. They depend on imports to cover 50 percent of their caloric intake, and by 2030 imports will cover two-thirds of their caloric intake. Subsidies for bread, sugar, cooking oil, and tea are supporting a rapid increase in demand. With current policies, cereal imports in the region will increase by 55 percent over the next two decades. Egypt's cereal imports will increase by 100 percent. All countries in the region aim to raise food self-sufficiency, but this cannot be achieved by increasing production only. There is a clear need to rationalize demand, which can be helped by reducing generalized food subsidies. Overconsumption of subsidized cereals, oil, and sugar also means underconsumption of other, healthier foods, with a negative impact on nutrition. Obesity, the high intake of animal fat, and the low intake of dietary fiber are risk factors for chronic noncommunicable diseases. Today the obesity rate in Egypt is 40 percent, which is higher than in the United States (33 percent).[4]

A large part of food subsidies is diverted away from their intended use of reducing hunger. There is tremendous waste along the supply chain of subsidized food. Subsidized bread is used as animal or fish feed, and subsidized oil and sugar is often sold on the black market. It is estimated that 28 percent of food subsidies in Egypt never reach their intended beneficiaries. Moreover, as in

3 Energy Sector Management Assistance Program and World Bank, (2009), Final Report: Consulting Services for an Energy Pricing Strategy in Egypt (Washington, DC: ESMAP).

4 Food and Agriculture Organization, Nutrition Country Profile, Egypt, accessed at ftp://ftp.fao.org/es/esn/nutrition/ncp/egy.pdf; Centers for Disease Control and Prevention, U.S. Obesity Trends, accessed at http://www.cdc.gov/obesity/data/trends.html.

the case of fuel subsidies, a large part of untargeted food subsidies go to the richest groups. In Egypt, the richest quintile receive about 12.6 percent more in absolute benefits from food subsidies than the poorest quintile.[5]

A system that replaces the current energy and food subsidies with direct income transfers to the poor will be fairer and more efficient. However, Arab regimes have so far been unable to make such a change. It is possible. Iran was able to reduce its subsidies in December 2010, quadrupling the price of gasoline in one day. Indonesia also implemented a bold energy subsidy reform program in 2005 and 2008. It remains to be seen whether the new governments resulting from the Arab Spring will be able to build the necessary consensus to bring about such a major policy change. They should strive for a progression from blanket subsidies to targeted subsidies and then to social investment, encouraging the economic mobility of low-income families.

The Housing Market

Housing policies under the old social contract further marginalized youth. Again using Egypt as an example, the introduction of rent control laws in the 1960s provided indefinite access to cheap housing for those who already had it but led to the virtual disappearance of rental housing from the formal housing market. Without significant cash up front to afford to purchase a unit or to buy into a rent control contract, the only option was the exploding informal housing market. Out of concern for the rapid expansion of informal settlements and the political threat they represented, the Egyptian regime began to crack down on informal housing in the early 1990s, reducing its

5 World Bank, (2005), *Egypt—Towards a More Effective Social Policy: Subsidies and Social Safety Nets* (Washington, DC: World Bank).

supply and further driving up its price. The shortage and high cost of housing in Egypt contributed to an increasing cost of marriage and a perception that the country was in the midst of a marriage crisis.[6] The median age of entering into a first marriage for men in Egypt rose from 27 for those born in 1960 to 29 for those born in 1972.[7]

The housing reforms introduced by the Egyptian government in 1996 brought some relief to the deteriorating housing situation for young people. A new housing law allowed for finite-duration housing contracts that were not subject to rent control. Although the law maintained rent control in all contracts signed prior to its adoption, it resulted in a significant increase in the supply of rental housing. Assaad and Ramadan (2008) show that this improved supply actually resulted in a decline in the median age of marriage for young men in Egypt after the passage of the new law.

Access to affordable housing for young people in Egypt and elsewhere in the Arab world continues to be constrained by the virtual absence of affordable financing for housing. Estimated at around 7 percent in Egypt and Algeria and 10 percent in Tunisia, mortgage finance constitutes a very small share of total credit in Arab countries.[8] Although a mortgage law was passed by the Egyptian parliament in 2001, it has been essentially ineffective in creating a meaningful housing finance sector to date because of a number of continuing structural challenges. The most serious of

6 D. Singerman and B. Ibrahim, (2001), "The Cost of Marriage in Egypt: A Hidden Variable in the New Arab Demography and Poverty Research," in N. Hopkins, ed., Special Edition on "The New Arab Family," *Cairo Papers in the Social Sciences* 24 (Spring): 80–116.

7 Ragui Assad and Mohamed Ramadan, (2008), "Did Housing Policy Reforms Curb the Delay in Marriage among Young Men in Egypt?" *Middle East Youth Initiative Policy Outlook*, no. 1. (Washington, DC: Brookings Institution, Wolfensohn Center for Development; Dubai School of Government).

8 Djavad Salehi-Isfahani and Navtej Dhillon, (2008), "Stalled Youth Transitions in the Middle East: A Framework for Policy Reform," *Middle East Youth Initiative Working Paper* 8 (Washington, DC: Brookings Institution, Wolfensohn Center for Development; Dubai School of Government).

these challenges are the cumbersome and ineffective legal frameworks governing property registration and collateral foreclosure
procedures.[9]

Other challenges include a lack of long-term financing to lend-
ers, an absence of a credit information system, and an inconsistent
approach to property valuation.[10] Although some progress has been
made to address these challenges in recent years, mortgage finance,
especially to low- and middle-income groups, remains highly
inaccessible. Through its national housing program launched in
2005, the Egyptian government has relied on direct and indirect
subsidies to the housing sector channeled primarily through public
sector providers as its main way to increase the supply of affordable housing. These subsidies are often poorly targeted and do not
contribute much to the development of a dynamic housing market.
A subsidy system targeted directly at qualifying individuals through
the mortgage finance system or through "sites and services" self-help
housing programs is more likely to reach the intended beneficiaries
and encourage a private sector supply response. In the meantime,
considerably more could be done to reduce the legal and bureaucratic obstacles standing in the way of a more inclusive mortgage
finance system.

PUBLIC SECTOR EMPLOYMENT

There are many reasons to rationalize the role of the public sector in
Arab labor markets. The best-known, and the subject of past reform

9 Sahar Nasr, (2010), "Financial Leasing in MENA Region: An Analysis of Financial,
Legal and Institutional Aspects," *Economic Research Forum Working Paper* 0424, available
at http://www.erf.org.eg/CMS/uploads/pdf/0424_final.pdf.

10 Stephen Everhart, Berta Heybey, and Patrick Carleton, (2006), "Egypt: Overview
of the Housing Sector," *Housing Finance International* 20(4): 9–15.

efforts, is the financial burden placed on the government and the rest of the economy by high public sector employment. Arab governments continue to employ a higher share of the population than any other developing region. This remains a concern, with government wage bills averaging 11.3 percent of the GDP in the late 1990s and reaching fiscally unsustainable levels in several oil-exporting countries. Despite reform efforts over the past decade, only a few countries reduced the size of the public sector wage bill, and in many countries the wage bill has increased. Wage expenditures are a significant drain on fiscal revenues, reducing the resources available for other sectors of the economy and potentially crowding out spending and investment by the private sector.

Efficiency losses due to falling productivity in the public sector are another concern. Across the Arab region, most branches of the public sector remain overstaffed even in countries that have tried to shed public sector labor. In the early 1990s, the share of underutilized workers in the public sector ranged from 17 percent in Algeria to 21 percent in Egypt to even higher shares among the oil-exporting countries. These estimates suggest that the scale of overstaffing is greater than ever. Some estimates put labor redundancies in public enterprises at approximately 35 percent in Egypt and nearly 40 percent in Jordan.[11] In Algeria, redundancy remains a concern despite layoffs of more than a half million workers during the 1990s.

Reducing Unemployment

Significant financial savings and efficiency gains would result from rationalizing public sector employment. These considerations alone

11 Elizabeth Ruppert Bulmer, (2002), "The Public Sector as Dominant Employer in MENA" (Washington DC: World Bank).

would justify scaling back the state's presence in labor markets. Of even more importance, the dominance of the public sector is linked to the structure of unemployment and the supply of skills in the economy. The need for public sector reform stems less from financial and overstaffing implications and more from the rigidities that state dominance introduces to labor markets. The perpetuation of implicit and explicit employment guarantees in government hiring and mismatched wage expectations resulting from generous public sector compensation policies create market segmentation and ensure a continued high demand for public sector jobs, especially among educated first-time job seekers.

In some countries, workers prefer government jobs because wages are higher than in the private sector. In other countries, workers are attracted to such nonwage factors as job security, worker protections, and social allowances unlinked to productivity.[12] These considerations, as well as special provisions on work hours and maternity leave, make public sector employment especially attractive to women. Large nonwage benefits, while a mechanism for distributing wealth, are distortionary, contributing to structural rigidities that reinforce the segmented structure of employment. In the labor-importing countries, public-private segmentation resulting from wage and nonwage advantages for nationals in the public sector is further reinforced by distinctions in employment between nationals and expatriates. Private sector wages are considerably lower in countries that rely on foreign laborers not covered by social protection legislation and benefits. At such low wage levels, nationals are often not willing to work, so mostly foreign workers are employed in the private sector.

---

12 World Bank MENA Development Report, (2004), *Unlocking the Employment Potential in the Middle East and North Africa: Toward a New Social Contract* (Washington DC: World Bank).

Policy Options

Policy makers have several instruments for reducing public employment, containing the public wage bill, and, most important, directing new labor market entrants toward private sector employment.[13] To be most effective and sustainable in the long run, the realignment of incentives to work in the private sector should rely on both push-and-pull factors. The menu of policies range from natural attrition and hiring freezes to accelerated attrition through substantial wage adjustments or benefit cuts to explicit retrenchment through layoffs. Because these options imply tradeoffs between the costs and benefits to workers and the public sector over different time periods, they may be introduced separately, sequentially, or simultaneously. The optimal combination of policies would vary by initial conditions, specific objectives, and the considerations of the political economy of labor markets.

Natural attrition rates can be high as employees leave public employment for private sector jobs or withdraw from the labor force because of disability, retirement, or for other reasons. The demographics of public employment can provide some notion of natural outflow rates. In Egypt and Morocco, for example, nearly 15 percent of public sector employees are more than 50 years old, and in Bahrain, Kuwait, and Oman, the equivalent figure is 10 percent. The average age of public sector employees is also rising as the influx of younger workers has decelerated. Thus, there is significant potential for employment reductions as staff members retire over the next 10 years. Combined with a hiring freeze, attrition alone could translate into substantially reduced employment levels in the public sector.

---

13 Martin Rama, (1999), "Efficient Public Sector Downsizing," World Bank Working Paper 1840 (Washington DC: World Bank).

Reducing remuneration can accelerate the process of attrition and shift a greater supply of labor to the private sector. Lower compensation in the public sector raises the appeal of private sector employment for both job seekers, as the reservation wage falls, and current employees, as the wage differential with the private sector shifts. Since cutting the wages of existing employees is likely to be politically difficult, especially when applied to tenured civil servants, alternative measures may be needed to reduce government employment and the wage bill. These include lowering remuneration for new entrants, adjusting the pay scale to strengthen the link between compensation and productivity, and focusing on nonwage benefits that distort labor decisions, such as generous pension systems and family allowances that add to the lure of employment in the public sector.

Algeria, for example, has no ceiling on the number of dependents eligible for family allowances, which in Kuwait is five dependents. The effects of these policies are distortionary, since workers can increase their remuneration by increasing family size rather than by increasing productivity. The nonwage benefit premium in the public sector represents a significant share of total public sector compensation (up to 50 percent) and represents the only variable that can be manipulated to reduce total compensation other than nominal wage cuts and pay scale reforms.

While lowering public sector remuneration can induce labor reallocation in the private sector through the price mechanism, public sector downsizing can also be facilitated through layoffs or voluntary separations. Most Arab countries have enabling legislation or precedents for such an approach. Because laid-off workers and dependents incur income losses through no fault of their own, for broader economic reasons, retrenchment is typically accompanied by some income support to smooth consumption over the period of joblessness. Severance packages also reward workers for years of past service. In addition to these equity and social protection considerations, there are macroeconomic stabilizing effects from severance packages as well, since large-scale layoffs lead to declines in income that depress aggregate demand. Most Arab countries have some type of severance requirement.

Compensation can take the form of severance pay delivered in a lump sum or in periodic payments, as is common in OECD countries. Lump-sum severance involves high upfront costs to employers, which may discourage layoffs. In Algeria, for example, until 1994 the law required employers to compensate laid-off workers with one month's salary per year of tenure (up to 15 months) in a lump-sum payment. Iran and Tunisia have legislation covering unemployment assistance, but only Algeria and Egypt have unemployment insurance in which formal sector workers participate through a mandatory payroll tax. In Egypt, there has been only modest use of this legislation because layoffs are allowed only when an enterprise is liquidated. Thus, within the Arab world, only Algeria has a functioning unemployment insurance system under which significant retrenchment has occurred.

GETTING GOOD GOVERNMENT

There is considerable variance in the quality of state institutions across the region. A large institutional gap exists between the richer Gulf countries, on the one hand, and countries such as Yemen and Libya, on the other. Such differences throughout the Arab world are exemplified by the variance in the quality of the public sector bureaucracy in formulating and implementing policies and delivering services. Although the Arab states, on average, saw a modest improvement in government effectiveness relative to other regions, this reflects both improvements in several countries and deteriorations in others. There are large differences among countries in the quality of regulatory regimes. The dimensions of rule of law and the control of corruption exhibit somewhat lower regional variation, but most Arab countries rate mediocre to poor in these categories.

Assessing Institutional Performance

The differences among countries on various institutional dimensions suggest that it would be misleading to generalize the situation and outlook across the region, even though, on average, governmental performance and the control of corruption among Arab states is low and the region lacks examples of countries that have improved in these respects.

Arab countries rate poorly in terms of the measures of government effectiveness that capture perceptions of the quality of public services, the quality of the civil service and the degree of its independence from political pressures, the quality of policy formulation and implementation, and the credibility of the government's commitment to such policies (Figure 4.3). In general, the "soft," demand-side aspects of government effectiveness—such as trust in government, consistency of policy direction, consensus building, and public satisfaction with services—have performed less well than such supply-side aspects as measures of the quality of regulatory agencies and the competence of bureaucratic administration. Within the Arab world, Libya and Yemen (as well as Iraq) stand out as having particularly poorly functioning governments. On a more positive note, Bahrain, Tunisia, Jordan, and Morocco have above-average government effectiveness. The issue there is more how to mobilize the machinery of government toward better and fairer outcomes rather than reforming or rebuilding existing government bureaucracies.

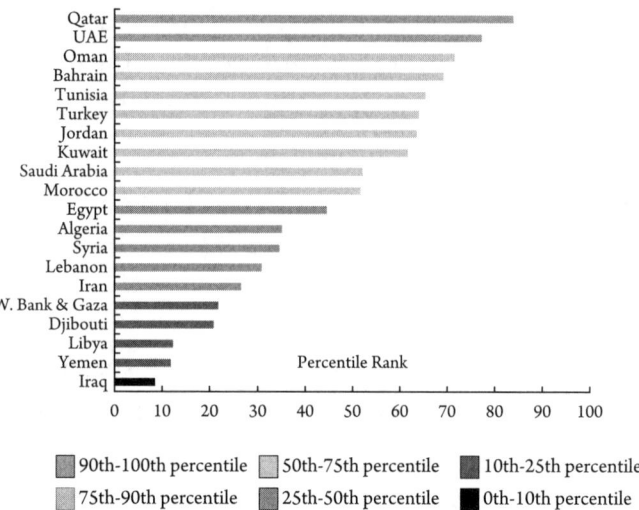

Qatar
UAE
Oman
Bahrain
Tunisia
Turkey
Jordan
Kuwait
Saudi Arabia
Morocco
Egypt
Algeria
Syria
Lebanon
Iran
W. Bank & Gaza
Djibouti
Libya
Yemen
Iraq

Percentile Rank

0 10 20 30 40 50 60 70 80 90 100

☐ 90th-100th percentile ☐ 50th-75th percentile ☐ 10th-25th percentile
☐ 75th-90th percentile ☐ 25th-50th percentile ■ 0th-10th percentile

Figure 4.3. Government Effectiveness in the Arab World, 2009. (*Source:* D. Kaufmann, A. Kraay, and M. Mastruzzi. *Worldwide Governance Indicators: A Summary of Data, Methodology and Analytical Issues.* Worldwide Governance Indicators Project, 2010, available at www.govindicators.org.)

Rebuilding Public Institutions

The critical weaknesses in Arab governance center on voice and accountability. Arab states have provided few avenues for meaningful participation of newly mobilized groups. This political gap must be closed for any fiscal reforms—or for any economic reforms, for that matter—to be sustained. Absent broad-based inclusion of previously disenfranchised groups, any reforms enacted will continue to require continuous negotiation with rulers, leaving reforms subject to problems of factionalism and credibility and—as has occurred during past economic reform attempts—reversal. Reformers' best intentions, therefore, risk being thwarted unless constituencies are able to access organizational resources, are able to articulate their interests collectively, are able to enforce accountability on leadership, and ultimately, are governed by state institutions that operate independently of individual rulers.

Reformers must be able to draw on and secure organized support. Increasing the organizational resources of groups that owe their wealth not to the privileges, spoils, or rents granted by incumbent regimes but to independent economic activity will increase the political weight of a constituency that naturally demands delineated property rights, curbs on executive discretion, greater professionalism and meritocracy in government. In parallel with promoting diversification, investment, and entrepreneurship— and thus creating new economic interests—boosting the power of reformers means enabling the development of political parties, employers' associations, professional associations, industry confederations, trade unions, civil society organizations, and other "peak," national-level organizations in countries in transitional or post-transitional phases.

Organizing support for reforms will require legal changes to permit independent labor unions and professional associations to form and operate without state approval. Without institutionalized political groupings capable of making broadly credible promises to citizens, the only policies that citizens can directly connect to government performance are the watered-down subsidies and guarantees that have become a mainstay of the social contract. It will be difficult for any democratic successor governments to unwind these specialized benefits in favor of broad-based measures, such as improving service delivery, without the presence of active political organizations.

In the medium term, the rudimentary organizations that emerge from the transitional period will require significant organizational assistance and financial support, some of which can be externally provided. But this expanded locus of organizational life will not sustain reforms without greater transparency and stronger lines of accountability to decision makers. Several Arab countries may be favorably disposed to embark on wide-ranging transparency-enhancing initiatives including freedom-of-information laws and public disclosure/public debate requirements for budgets and for all laws prior to their passage. Transparency can also be enhanced through improved public financial management and procurement practices, as in Tunisia, for example. These efforts should be applauded.

In addition, stronger accountability via increasing the capacity of legislatures, courts, local governments, supreme audit institutions, subnational governments, and other bodies is another area for attention. These efforts will have to go hand in hand with organizational capacity building. In Morocco and Jordan, monarchs are using the absence of effective political organizations as justification for retaining tight control over palace-led efforts to increase transparency and accountability. Jordan's Abdullah II, after agreeing to protestors' demands that future prime ministers be appointed and dismissed by parliament rather than by the king, later rejected this because of the lack of mature parties.[14] Meanwhile, Morocco's Mohammed IV has closely managed a constitutional reform commission from the palace, with some, albeit insufficient, participation of political parties, labor unions, civic groups, and other organizations in the process.[15]

Ultimately, institutional and economic reforms can only be recoupled by reversing the long period of state deinstitutionalization that has proceeded in the Arab world. The absence of a political basis for sustainable economic reforms has been a deliberate objective of partial autocracies in the region, and thus true change requires that Arab leaders redefine the relationship between the state and its citizens. The rebuilding of political organizations and the enhancing of formal and legal transparency and accountability

14 Rami G. Khouri, (2011), "Jordan as a Test Case," *Middle East Online*, available at http://www.middle-east-online.com/english/?id=46810.

15 "Morocco's Monarchy: Reform or Fall," *The Economist* (April 20, 2011), available at http://www.economist.com/ node/18587225.

are initial and intermediate steps. In the long term, however, the rebuilding of the capacity, professionalism, and integrity of state institutions will emerge as a vital component of any transition in the Arab world.

Selectivity in Public Sector Reform

Many of the public sector reforms previously described are long term in nature. Where should governments start? One possible answer is to pay close attention to public opinion polls on the level of satisfaction with public services. These polls should be done in each country on a scientific basis, but as an example of the kind of results that might be expected, one can use international polls that look at a few of the main public services. Figure 4.4 shows that in Egypt, particular attention should be paid to affordable housing and preservation of the environment (garbage collection and sanitation). The same poll also shows that the rate of deterioration of satisfaction with public transport was highest between 2009 and 2010, suggesting that that sector also should not be neglected. In Tunisia, satisfaction levels are generally higher than in Egypt, but housing, roads, and health care stand out as having witnessed sharp deterioration in 2010. Given that these polls are not comprehensive across the range of all public services, they cannot be taken as the basis for policymaking, but they do suggest that there is important information on public satisfaction that should feed into the prioritization of policies and institutional reforms that should be reflected in national budgets.

National Dialogue

The main motivation behind the Arab Spring was neither political nor exclusively economic. It was mainly a call for human rights and

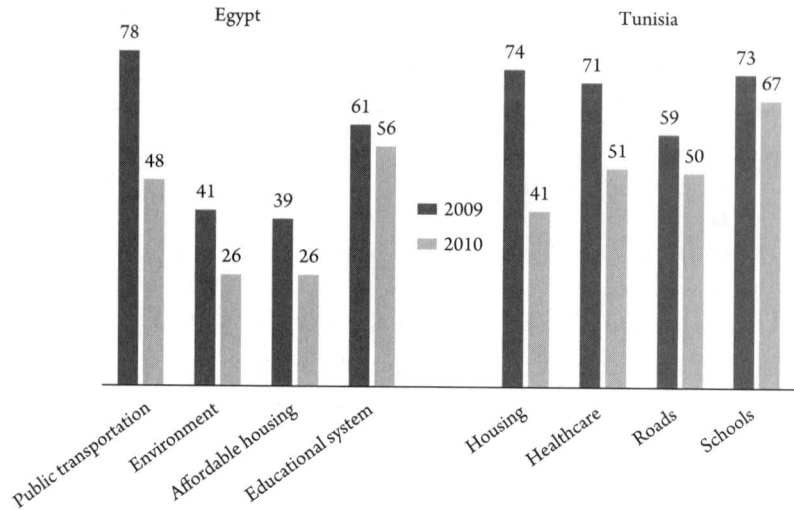

Figure 4.4. Satisfaction with Government-Provided Social Services in Egypt and Tunisia. (*Sources:* Gallup Inc. "Egypt: The Arithmetic of Revolution." Abu Dhabi: Gallup Inc., 2011; Gallup Inc. "Tunisia: Analyzing the Dawn of the Arab Spring." Abu Dhabi: Gallup Inc.)

dignity. Protesters wanted their rights to be protected, respected, and equally treated as individuals and citizens. They were also fighting against corruption, exclusion, and marginalization. People wanted to feel involved in their country's development plan to claim a position as the target of this development.

Without strong institutions and representative civil society bodies, the process of policymaking in Arab Spring economies must rely on new types of consultations. In Egypt, the military council established a panel of 10 distinguished independent citizens to debate five transitional issues: political, economic, social, media and culture, and foreign relations. A national conference sparked a debate in plenary and parallel sessions that involved a broad range of stakeholders. Similar events were undertaken at the subnational level. A healthy process of stakeholder inclusion in economic policy debate was started.

Such a national dialogue between citizens and their state should be encouraged. Dialogues work best when they have precise objectives and outputs in which people feel actively involved in shaping policy. But success is not automatic; several dialogues in the region have failed because of open-ended agendas lacking specificity and follow-up or because those engaged in the dialogue were not representative of broader stakeholders.

A dialogue is an ongoing process that should be conducted in more than one stage. It should make an effort to combine political, economic, and social issues in a holistic way. Often, local development issues are more relevant to the immediate living standards of the people. At local levels, it is easier for the state to lead a discussion of citizen's needs and of the roles and responsibilities of various organizations. Concrete results, such as the gradual capacity building of citizen organizations, can be more easily achieved.

The outcome of the dialogue could be an agenda for a reform plan and a road map in which the rights, obligations, and responsibilities of citizens, government, private sector, and civil society could be defined and activated in a gradual manner.

There are many different ways for organizing a national dialogue. Each country must choose its own way. In some settings, however, it seems that a dialogue can help improve perceptions and attitudes toward reform, even if results on the ground take longer to materialize. One example is Indonesia. There, surveys found that satisfaction with public services was far higher after a decentralization program, even though actual indicators of service delivery appeared not to have improved. The process was the difference.

Box 4.1 LESSONS FROM INDONESIA'S TRANSITION

Indonesia is widely considered as having had a successful transition after its economic crisis in 1998. Like many countries in the Arab world, it had high public debt levels, large subsidies, rampant corruption, crony capitalism, and weak institutions. It took seven years for the GDP per capita to return to precrisis levels. What accounts for Indonesia's relative success?

The government in Indonesia knew that it would be difficult to deliver economic improvements in the short term. Poverty rates initially soared. Leaders sought to deliver process changes that would involve the citizenry more directly in economic policymaking. These process changes included:

- A major decentralization law to bring public services closer to the people, that was swiftly implemented ("big bang"), despite the reservations of external advisers concerned over technical details.
- A new partnership—the Partnership for Governance Reform—between the government and civil society to lead the fight against corruption.
- New laws allowing the police to investigate corruption, followed by the establishment of a Corruption Eradication Commission (KPK).
- The blossoming of civil society organizations.
- The development of a free and vibrant press.
- The formation of an independent Socioeconomic Monitoring and Research Unit (SMERU) to provide objective analysis of socioeconomic and poverty issues and policies.

With these process changes, along with political reforms, the Indonesian citizenry became more deeply and passionately involved in their own development. They felt empowered. Many individuals were able to take actions that made a difference. Over time, the process changes also delivered tangible results. For example, SMERU was able to design the highly successful program for targeted compensation funding when fuel subsidies were reduced in 2005. KPK enjoyed many notable successes in bringing cases against corrupt officials, but the most significant achievement was the cumulative engagement of Indonesian citizens in their country's development.

Chapter 5

TRANSFORMING THE PRIVATE SECTOR

Since the beginning of the Arab Spring, discussions of private-sector reform imperatives in the Arab world have been dramatically changed by events. Countries such as Egypt, Libya, and Tunisia that are entering transitional periods have little choice but to unlock the potential of their private sectors to create jobs, attract investment, and to take steps toward developing globally competitive economies. Countries in which rulers continue to survive, similarly, have little choice but to address long-term causes of public anger—in particular, a persistent lack of good job opportunities (especially among the young and other marginalized groups)—alongside the sources of other political frustrations.

The challenge facing Arab economies is that, while the private sector is essential to growth and employment, it is also seen as party to the corruption and inequities that prevailed in the old order. In this regard, the context in the Arab world is similar to that in East Asian countries faced with a crisis on crony capitalism in 1997 and 1998. Efforts to aggressively pursue past corruption in the name of justice risk alienating large entrepreneurs, chilling the investment climate, and precipitating capital flight. Administrators have frozen approval processes for investments out of concern for the potential for future investigation. But condoning past corruption would send the wrong "business as usual" signals and generate moral hazard. Finding the right balance will not be easy.

The private sector in the Arab world is saddled with a number of problems. Arab economies enjoy less competition than other regions. Firms tend to be older and less competitive than their counterparts in Asia, Latin America, or eastern Europe. New firms find it harder to enter markets, and inefficient firms are less likely to exit. As such, the dynamism and innovation that companies bring—the "creative destruction" process so essential to productivity—is occurring at a much less rapid pace. The response of private investment to past reforms has been weaker than in other regions.[1] The ratio of private to public investment is far lower than in other regions. To make matters worse, in the wake of the Arab Spring, key industries such as tourism, construction, retail, and banking have been deeply affected, while trade flows and lines of credit have been curtailed. Labor strikes and protests set back a number of industries, further disrupting economic activity. The Institute for International Finance estimates that $16 billion was withdrawn by investors from Egypt in the first quarter after the revolution. The foreign reserve position of the central bank remains comfortable for the time being but has seen substantial decline.

To boost employment and sustain growth, the Arab world needs more high value added firms, ranging from agroprocessing to manufacturing to tradable services. These are precisely the industries that have bypassed the region in the past 15 to 20 years. Whether judged by the diversification of industry and exports, technological sophistication, the level and sectoral composition of private investment, or the productivity and innovation of firms, the Arab world has not undergone the kind of economic transformation seen in countries that have successfully sustained growth and job creation.

1 World Bank, (2009), *From Privilege to Competition: Unlocking Private-Led Growth in the Middle East and North Africa* (Washington, DC: World Bank).

A STRUCTURAL DEFICIT IN THE NONOIL SECTOR

The Arab private sector largely consists of microenterprises, livelihood businesses, and small and medium enterprises (SMEs). Perhaps 26 million adults participate in some form of entrepreneurial activity, including nearly 6 million in Egypt alone, according to a recent representative survey.[2] The vast majority of these small firms has less than five employees, is family owned, and has little to do with the sectors that have been the subject of official policy initiatives.

The private sector primarily serves local markets. The Arab region's nonoil exports represent less than 1 percent of world trade, which is the lowest share of any developing region. The low ratio of nonenergy exports to GDP among countries in the Arab region is among the clearest signs of a lack of global competitiveness and indicates that a key potential source of job creation has not been tapped. A few countries, such as Morocco, have made tangible steps toward penetrating the European market, but with very few products relative to its GDP, as a whole the region is far below its potential.

While a number of factors have contributed to this poor export performance, analysts cite high average tariffs, behind the border investment climate constraints, and the low quality of Arab-produced goods.[3] Low-performing transport infrastructures and the low quality of services in many countries of the region have

2 International Development Research Center, (2010), *Global Entrepreneurship Monitor, Middle East and North Africa (GEM-MENA)*, (Ottawa: IDRC). The survey was based on Saudi Arabia, Turkey, UAE, Syria, West Bank/Gaza, Tunisia, Iran, Egypt, Jordan, Lebanon, Morocco, Algeria, and Yemen.

3 Mustapha Kemal Nabli, (2007), *Breaking the Barriers to Higher Economic Growth: Better Governance and Deeper Reforms in the Middle East and North Africa* (Washington DC: World Bank).

adversely affected trade flows through higher costs, delays, and uncertainty, along with low productivity. For some countries, particularly Algeria and Libya, high labor costs, the high costs of nontradables, and overvalued exchange rates combine with a dominant state enterprise sector and a restrictive regulatory environment to create limited prospects for nonoil exports.

A Burdensome Policy Environment

The overarching feature of the business environment in the Arab region is a complex structure of administrative controls that remain as a legacy of state-directed development. In the course of implementation and enforcement, this structure has created a logjam of overlapping requirements, prevented transparency, and created conditions for corruption and excessive administrative discretion. In the most common institutional model in the region, the presidency is the authority that issues the most important regulations, but many others are issued at the ministerial level, by parliaments, or, where relevant, through guidance from the crown. The combination of new orders, decrees, and regulations, mixed with previously issued ones that are not typically withdrawn, has created overlaps of authority and confusion and frustration for the private sector. The Egypt Regulatory Reform and Development Activity (ERRADA) has identified and catalogued more than 36,000 regulations from 10 ministries. In Tunisia, a recent effort has quickly catalogued more than 500 regulations in the Ministry of Finance alone, and the ministry is now taking steps to remove all except those supported by law or necessity.

These requirements, and the resulting opacity, have undermined policy. Firms in Egypt have consistently highlighted the need to address corruption and to encourage greater transparency and accountability, while reducing the incentives and scope for bureaucratic discretion and informality.[4] Macroeconomic uncertainty, regulatory policy uncertainty, informal competition, and corruption were identified as four of the top five constraints on firms in the World Bank's 2009 Egypt Investment Climate Assessment: Forty-three percent of surveyed firms said that officials expected an informal payment or gift to get a construction permit. More than half of hotels reported such payments to get an import card; twenty-six percent of manufacturers and 33 percent of services providers report the need for informal payments for access to running water. These results are consistent with evidence from around the world indicating that excessive, top-down regulations increase corruption, raise costs for the private sector, reduce the ability to create jobs, and force firms into the informal sector where they do not pay taxes.

Many reforms are well designed but not implemented at the point of contact with the private sector. A telling example is the modern building code that Egypt has introduced. It would sharply reduce the number of onsite inspections which the private sector reports is a cause of informal payments. These inspections are undertaken by officials from governorates and new urban communities. However, the private sector reports that these levels of government are still subjecting industry to the same inspections and procedures, despite the new law. A vertical coordination of policy across levels of government is missing.

In some countries, the control mechanism to ensure proper implementation of the law is through accountability to local communities, which can be enhanced by the use of citizen scorecards and other forms of monitoring. In the current environment, federal-local relationships are not clear, and the local capacity

---

4 World Bank, (2009), *Egypt Investment Climate Assessment 2009: Accelerating Private Enterprise-Led Growth* (Washington, DC: World Bank).

to enforce delegated responsibilities is weak. As a consequence, the response to several reforms has sometimes been to introduce additional control mechanisms that then result in a further administrative burden on private firms.

A Financial Sector That Benefits Few

Financial intermediation by the banking system is weak by international standards. Most of the credit extended to the private sector goes to a small number of large firms with most firms, especially small and medium enterprises (SMEs), receiving little financing from banks. Policies governing the financial sector also reduce private sector efficiency and favor resource allocation to large firms. Only 20 percent of SMEs have access to finance, a level far lower than other regions, except for Africa, and the share of the population covered by microfinance is half that of Latin America. On the other hand, large firms have perhaps excessive access to finance. Arab banks have the highest average loan concentration ratio in the world, at 242 percent, as measured by their exposure to the 20 largest borrowers as a share of total equity.

The causes are several. Competition in the financial sector between banks and between banking and nonbanking sources of finance is limited. The Egyptian financial system, for example, has suffered from significant entry and exit barriers; as a result competition was limited and inefficient banks were allowed to continue operating. State-owned banks, which dominate the banking system, lag in efficiency and in risk management practices compared to their private counterparts.

A modest shift in market share from state banks to private banks is a step in the right direction, but the financial sectors of the Arab world remain less competitive than those in other regions, due to stricter barriers to entry, weak credit information systems, and the lack of competition from capital markets and nonbanking institutions.[5]

In any economy, it is hard for the private sector to develop without reliable institutions that address market failures, including in the financial sector. Arab countries are still overly dependent on public registries with limited coverage and poor quality of information. Collateral regimes are limited in the type of assets that may be used as collateral, enforcing security interests takes a long time, and in a bankruptcy, secured creditors do not have a sufficiently clear priority. The region ranks last in a ranking of the legal rights of creditors in the World Bank's Doing Business Index.[6] Overall, the Arab financial infrastructure is poor.

Meanwhile, insolvency regimes are largely in their infancy. Bankruptcy is considered a criminal offense in several Arab countries, and business failure is associated with considerable personal stigma, thus creating a strong disincentive for entrepreneurship. In Tunisia, these weaknesses were circumvented by the creation of an effective offshore regime to attract foreign investment, but that in turn has prevented effective linkages with the domestic economy.

A Failure to Industrialize

The impact of a small, informal private sector and a burdensome regulatory environment can be seen in the partial and incomplete development of the non–oil sector. Economies that have successfully generated growth in output and employment and made the transition from low-income to high-income status typically have experienced significant changes in their economic structure.

5 World Bank, (2011), *Financial Access and Stability: A Roadmap for the MENA Region* (Washington, DC: World Bank).

6 World Bank, Doing Business Indicator, www.doingbusiness.org/rankings.

Although structural transformation has been under way in Arab economies for at least four decades, the region's current economic structure differs significantly from comparable middle-income countries. Taking as a benchmark the structural characteristics of a sample of non-Arab countries at the time at which they crossed over from lower- to upper-middle-income economies, the small share of manufacturing in total output is both striking and worrisome.[7]

The sectoral shares of value added for selected Arab countries appear in Table 5.1 along with the simple average of the benchmark middle-income countries. Even Tunisia, the region's industrial success story, trails the benchmark by nearly 12 percentage points of its GDP in its share of manufacturing. Limited evidence suggests that the share of manufacturing in total employment, as well as the volume of employment in the manufacturing sector, has been stagnant in Arab economies since the 1990s.[8]

Agriculture constitutes a larger portion of the economy in Arab economies than in the benchmark, and it continues to employ large numbers. This also reflects the slow progress of structural change in the region. The service sector is also larger than in the benchmark and has absorbed much of the increase in the labor force. Services in Arab economies are highly diverse, ranging from high productivity sectors, such as banking, insurance and finance, to low productivity street vendors. Employment in high productivity service activities has been growing very slowly in the last decade. Trade

7 Benchmark countries and years are: Brazil (2005), Chile (1995), China (2009), Malaysia (1995), Mauritius (2003), Thailand (2010), and Turkey (2004). The threshold income level for the benchmark countries is taken as $3,975 gross national income per capita in 2010 dollars. This level roughly corresponds to the average income of the region's lower middle-income countries—Egypt, Morocco, and Syria—and its upper-middle-income economies of Tunisia and Jordan.

8 Because of a lack of data on employment, it was not possible to estimate the employment shares for individual economies.

Table 5.1 ARAB COUNTRY STRUCTURAL DEFICIT 2005

	Value Added Share of Agriculture	Value Added Share of Manufacturing	Value Added Share of Services
Benchmark Middle-Income Country	8.7	28.1	49.3
Egypt	13.7	15.7	49.0
Morocco	16.4	15.9	55.1
Tunisia	7.8	16.5	62.3

Notes: Benchmark middle-income country as defined in text.

Sources: Margaret S. McMillan and Dani Rodrik, (2011), "Globalization, Structural Change and Productivity Growth," Working Paper 17143 (Cambridge, MA: National Bureau for Economic Research); Marcel P. Timmer and Gaaitzen J. de Vries, (2009), "Structural Change and Growth Accelerations in Asia and Latin America: A New Sectoral Data Set" *Cliometrica* 3 (2): 165-190.

and small-scale repair shops (motor as well as household goods) are the only service activities that have grown rapidly, but a large proportion of these activities in the labor-abundant economies are informal and characterized by low productivity and low wages.

The structural deficit mainly reflects a failure of Arab countries to industrialize. Table 5.2 presents some basic indicators of industrial development for the Arab region as a whole and for Egypt, Morocco, and Tunisia. The Arab states lag other developing countries in three measures of industrial dynamism. Manufacturing output per capita ranges from 53 percent of the developing country average for Morocco to slightly more than the global average for Tunisia. The region's share of manufacturing in its GDP is low, relative both to developing countries as a whole and, especially, to East Asia. Most disturbingly, the rate of growth of the manufacturing

Table 5.2 SELECTED INDICATORS OF INDUSTRIAL
DEVELOPMENT, 2005–2008

	Manufacturing Value Added Per Capita 2008 (US$)	Share of Manufacturing in GDP 2008 (%)	Rate of Change in Manufacturing Share of GDP 00–08
Arab Average	381.4	12.1	0.85
Egypt	278.9	15.7	−0.68
Morocco	219.0	15.9	−0.81
Tunisia	414.7	16.5	−1.12
Developing Countries	412.9	21.7	1.14
East Asia	632.5	29.5	1.49

Source: United Nations Industrial Development Organization, Industrial Statistics Database database; author's calculations.

share of value added is negative, indicating that the manufacturing sector is declining in relative importance in all three countries.

The global industrial economy has undergone major changes in the last quarter century. Developing countries—especially industrializing nations in East Asia—have become the center of global manufacturing. Between 2000 and 2008, manufacturing growth in industrialized economies was only about 1 percent per year; in developing economies it was more than 7 percent.[9] Arab economies—with the possible exception of Tunisia—largely missed the transformation of the global industrial economy. Whether they

9 UNIDO, (2009), *Industrial Development Report* (Geneva: United Nations Industrial Development Organization).

can now compete successfully to attract global industry is likely to depend on how well they are able to deal with four key drivers of global industrial location: trade in tasks, firm capabilities, agglomeration, and industry without smokestacks.

First, in many manufacturing activities the production process can be disaggregated into a series of steps, or tasks. As transport and coordination costs have fallen, it has become efficient for the production of different tasks to be located in different countries, each working on a different step. Task-based production has expanded dramatically in the past 20 years and has been a major driver of the rapid industrialization of the new generation of Asian export manufacturers. It has also propelled Tunisia's relative export success. Because task-based production is highly mobile, it represents an important first step through which countries can enter global value chains but also presents a challenge in retaining task-based investment.

Second, success in the global market depends on achieving a minimum competitive standard of productivity and quality. In most industries, these depend on a set of interlocking elements of tacit knowledge or working practices possessed jointly by the individuals who comprise the firm's workforce. These firm capabilities are the know-how or working practices that are used either in the course of production or in developing new products.[10] Low capability firms lack a mastery of the complex and interrelated bodies of knowledge and patterns of behavior that are needed to achieve competitiveness, and, because high capability firms tend to locate in environments that are rich in tacit knowledge, attracting high capability firms to low capability environments is difficult.

Third, manufacturing and service industries tend to concentrate in geographical areas—usually cities—driven by common needs

10 John Sutton, (2005), *Competing in Capabilities: An Informal Overview* (London School of Economics).

for raw materials, intermediate goods, access to markets, knowledge flows, and specialized skills.[11] Because of the productivity boost that agglomerations provide, locations that have achieved a critical mass of industry have a built-in advantage over new industrializers in attracting further industry. Starting a new industrial location is a form of collective action problem: If a critical mass of firms can be persuaded to locate in a new area, they will realize productivity gains, but no single firm has the incentive to locate in a new area in the absence of others.

Finally, manufacturing increasingly shares a broad range of characteristics with agroindustry and high value added, tradable services. Activities such as the global agricultural value chain in flowers and horticultural crops, remote services, or tourism require firm capabilities that differentiate them from traditional agriculture and services. Such industries without smokestacks offer countries an opportunity to expand the sources of growth-enhancing structural change.

Breaking In, Moving Up

Arab countries face at least three industrialization challenges, shaped by the way in which the income levels and factor endowments of its economies interact with the global determinants of industrial location. For the region's labor-abundant, resource-poor economies—such as Egypt and Morocco—the challenge of breaking into global markets in task-based production is likely to be the most urgent. The region's resource-poor middle-income economies—Jordan, Lebanon, and Tunisia—face the challenge of moving up the value chain, increasing exports by improving their

---

11 M. Fujita, P. Krugman, and A. J. Venables, (1990), *The Spatial Economy: Cities, Regions and International Trade* (Cambridge, MA: MIT Press).

product sophistication if they are going to compete globally. The oil exporters—the GCC countries, Algeria, and Iraq—confront a diversification challenge in the face of Dutch disease. Industry without smokestacks widens the scope of possibilities for attracting high value added industries for all three categories of countries.

Today, new manufacturing ventures are competing with East Asia, which now assumes the role previously played by the advanced economies of western Europe, the United States, and Japan. Asia has the scale and agglomeration economies that make it competitive against new entrants, despite rising production costs. One scenario, which cannot be wholly dismissed, is that the differences in wages between East Asia and the labor-abundant economies in countries such as Egypt may not be sufficiently large enough to offset East Asia's productivity advantage, making it impossible for Arab countries to compete. There are at least two reasons to think that the future is less bleak than this suggests. First, both real wages and congestion costs are rising in China, and second, growing domestic demand and policy responses to the global financial crisis have reoriented demand in Asia toward internal markets. These trends may provide a window of opportunity for labor-abundant, low-wage Arab economies.

For the region's upper-middle-income, non–oil economies, the industrial development challenge is somewhat different. Real wage levels are sufficiently high that, with the exception of Tunisia, they have not been attractive as final stage producers in task-based trade. At the same time, the region's nations, including Tunisia, have failed to keep pace with the rapidly growing industrial economies of Asia in more sophisticated industrial exports. This pressure in the middle has prevented Arab economies from making the transition from lower to higher sophistication manufacturing, limiting output and employment growth. The good news is that pressure in the middle is not uniform. Timeliness is emerging as a critical factor in the geographic distribution of global production. This may open up space for those economies with close proximity to Europe, such as Tunisia, to master more complex tasks as part of the global trend toward "reverse outsourcing."

Diversification is made difficult by the relative price changes that occur in a resource-exporting economy. Dutch disease cannot be avoided, but it can be addressed by public policy. Tradable goods production depends not only on the exchange rate but also on the investments and institutional innovations that governments make to enhance competitiveness. An effective diversification strategy, therefore, depends on identifying policy changes and investments that have a high likelihood of increasing firm-level productivity.

Guidelines for Industrial Development

Appropriate policy responses to the Arab countries' three industrialization challenges will vary. One set of public actions is cross-cutting. This includes mainly policies and investments directed at improving the investment climate: the regulatory, institutional, and physical environment within which firms operate. But investment climate reforms alone may not be sufficient. For countries to break in, move up, and diversify, strategic initiatives aimed at pushing exports, building capabilities, and supporting industrial clusters will be needed.

In all labor-abundant Arab economies, the export market represents the only option for rapid growth of manufacturing, agroindustry, and high value added services. Countries such as Egypt, Jordan, Morocco, and Syria face the challenge of breaking into the global market. Tunisia's export challenge is somewhat different. It needs to move from low-end final-stage assembly operations to more sophisticated exports. For this to occur, it will need to attract higher capability firms and facilitate the transfer of capabilities to domestic manufacturing.

In both cases, success in export markets in a world of task-based production and agglomeration will require more than piecemeal improvements in the investment climate. It will need an export push: a concerted set of public investments and policy and institutional reforms focused on increasing the share of industrial exports in the GDP. These initiatives will need to range from further efforts to reduce antiexport bias to the successful operation of export processing zones (EPZs) to institutional reforms and infrastructure investments aimed at improving trade logistics.

Capability building is complementary to the export push. All Arab economies need a strategy to attract high capability firms. Because foreign direct investment (FDI) is an effective means of introducing high capability firms into a lower capability environment, policies and institutions for attracting FDI are a key tool in capability building. Arab economies from the Gulf to Morocco have an unfinished agenda on the promotion of FDI. Autonomous, professional, and results-oriented FDI promotion agencies can make a major contribution to building capabilities in the region. Within an economy, vertical value chains are a major source of learning for firms. Removing obstacles to the formation of vertical value chain relationships should therefore be a major objective for public policies aimed at domestic capability building. Here again the challenges facing each Arab economy are distinct, but a central objective, equally valid in Egypt or Tunisia, should be to design an open architecture for special economic zones that permits free movement of labor, capital, management, and goods between the zone and the domestic economy. For Tunisia, in particular, a liberal offshore regime to attract FDI was not compatible with the excessive regulations governing the domestic economy, so that few firms benefiting from the FDI regime developed strong linkages with domestic suppliers.

Appropriate spatial policies to attract a critical mass of industry are likely to be a prerequisite to breaking into global markets. Case studies indicate that governments can foster industrial agglomerations by concentrating investment in high-quality institutions, social services, and infrastructure in a limited physical area such as a special economic zone (SEZ). In East Asia and Latin America, spatial policies have been explicitly linked to an export push through the use of export processing zones that are properly viewed as industrial agglomerations designed to serve the global market. The Arab world's experience with spatial industrial policies has been mixed. Tunisia's special economic zones appear to have been a partial success. Egypt's EPZs have generally been regarded as failures.

Because of the variety of industrialization challenges faced by the Arab economies, there is no single appropriate industrialization strategy for the region. It is likely that all three of the policy areas outlined here will need to be implemented in each country, but the nature of the policies will vary by the level of industrial development, the resource endowment, and the capabilities of enterprises in each country. Table 5.3 sets out a typology of industrialization challenges and strategies for three classes of Arab economies.

The most challenging reforms may be in rich countries trying to diversify. This will depend, to a great extent, on their ability to empower citizens with the required knowledge and their capacity to support innovation. These economies are challenged by an insufficiently trained workforce, unproductive SMEs, and weakness in innovation and entrepreneurship.

First, upgrading and enhancing workforce skills are essential measures to improve the capacity for competitiveness and to increase its productivity. Educational reforms, an emphasis on job training, and appropriate incentives are needed.

Second, SMEs are unproductive, in part, because they lack access to capital and to good infrastructure that tends to be

Table 5.3 INDUSTRIALIZATION CHALLENGES AND RESPONSES

	Breaking In	Moving Up	Diversifying
Country Examples	Egypt, Morocco	Lebanon, Tunisia	Algeria, Libya, GCC
Industrialization Challenge	Lower end task-based trade and agroindustry	Mastering more sophisticated products and tasks	Finding niche markets for high value-added manufacturing and services
Investment Climate Reforms	Regulation; trade-related infrastructure; skills	Regulation; trade-related infrastructure; skills	Regulation; skills
Strategic Components	Export Push; EPZs; Aggressive FDI policy	Spatial policies linking skills, knowledge, and capabilities; FDI; production knowledge initiatives	Linking industrialization to the resource; spatial policies linking skills, knowledge, and capabilities; production knowledge initiatives

concentrated in special zones. They also lack linkages to larger firms through value chains that could help them absorb new technologies and to innovate.

Third, innovation and entrepreneurship are limited because they rely on investments in developing the skills and advancing the knowledge of the workforce rather than just on investments in infrastructure, which have been comparatively easy to put in place.

A range of policy instruments is being experimented with across the region, in particular:

- investing in education, training, and educational development
- expanding SME's access to capital and technical assistance
- establishing entrepreneurship grants
- establishing microfinance schemes for small-scale startups and individuals
- creating venture capital funds, establishing and expanding business incubators, and investing in new technology startups
- partnering Arab countries with selected foreign "knowledge centers" to establish ties on innovation, education, and intellectual property
- initiating new sectors or clusters within a short period of time[12]

It is still too early to assess the cost benefit of these interventions, but it would be useful for countries in the region to pay close attention to these efforts and to exchange information about what works and under what circumstances. Such lessons would be easier

---

12 Nazar S. Al Baharna, Anil Khurana, and Martyn F. Roetter, (2006), *Creating a Knowledge-Based Society in Bahrain* (Bahrain: UNDP).

to develop if program evaluation were done in a systematic way across the region.

CAN THE ARAB WORLD COMPETE?

To many, the Arab private sector is seen as synonymous with corruption. Yet there is no sustainable response to the aspirations of youth without the private sector playing a leading role and without governments in the region taking needed steps to build confidence in the private sector. That requires a substantial reform agenda, including private sector leaders who focus on production and innovation, rather than on seeking rents. Reform must come from both directions. The public sector must give up control, and the private sector must concentrate on its productive capacity and not renew attempts at state capture.

Unless it is possible for enterprises to succeed without paying bribes, no amount of dialogue or prosecution will end the practice. For many small and microenterprises—including the self-employed, as in the case of Mohamed Bouazizi—with short-term funds borrowed at high interest rates, the option of waiting for long bureaucratic processes simply does not exist.

Governments are starting to take action, but more must be done. In Egypt, the prime minister recently removed requirements for new industrial projects to get approval, simplified the process of registering branches of foreign companies, removed the requirement for media companies to register with security services, made import certificates valid for three years rather than requiring frequent renewals, and established new branches of the Investment Authority. Tunisia, perhaps furthest along, has launched a regulatory "guillotine" process through which hundreds of obsolete regulations in the Ministry of Finance are being eliminated. Morocco has established the Comité National de l'Environnement des Affaires (CNEA), which has coordinated reform across ministries, leading to the nation being named the most improved investment climate in the annual Doing Business ratings. Most countries in the region could move to online registration of businesses, online payment of VAT and social insurance contributions, and combine tax and social insurance registration services at a single site.

None of these issues is new, and several previous efforts have been made at reform. But those have typically relied on the political will of an enlightened minister, president, or prime minister. They produced important results, but for the most part the effects were fleeting and reversible. In the case of Jordan, elites have blocked reform initiatives that would raise the quality of life for the average Jordanian but reduce the power of those elites, and this probably describes the situation in other countries as well.[13]

Past reform efforts, however well intentioned and initially successful, have mostly been weighed down and overcome by an administrative culture without modern alternatives, partial reform, and the strength of vested interests. For the private sector at the street level, the net result has been to reduce revenue and raise costs—a recipe for business failure, which under the current legislative regime in many countries of the region is a criminal offense. For governments, the net result has been to reduce the size of the formal private sector and, therefore, the tax base. Without tax revenues, public services and institutions suffer, civil service salaries are lower, and fresh incentives for corruption arise. While this was never the policy intent, the new governments in the region need to reverse these trends.

13 Marwan Muasher, (2011), *A Decade of Struggling Reform Efforts in Jordan: The Resilience of the Rentier System* (Washington, DC: Carnegie Endowment).

MOVING FORWARD WITH PRIVATE SECTOR REFORM

While governments have long voiced support for the private sector, this has been belied by significant government intervention in markets through public sector employment and state control of industry. The Arab world's traditional approach to economic management has offered a minority of workers security of employment but at the expense of declining wages and overall standards of living. It sustained redistributive policies that mitigate inequality but are underfunded and increasingly ineffective. Moreover, private sector reforms in the region have often produced backlashes against private investors and entrepreneurs rather than against the public policies that enabled the past abuses.

Conditions, of course, have changed dramatically in recent years. With fewer opportunities for labor migration, less regional circulation of oil revenues, and intense competition for foreign investment, Arab governments will increasingly depend on globally competitive domestic private sectors to sustain desirable social policies. To move the private sector reform process beyond its current limits, governments will need to revive national conversations about labor markets, service delivery, regulation, and the problems of cronyism. Governments will need to rebuild trust across the citizen sector and the private sector as part of a coalition for reform that is sustainable and built on mutual accountability. Governments will need to make strategic choices about their role and perform that role well while empowering other actors to also contribute to the transformation.

The Role of Public-Private Dialogue

Public-private dialogue is a key tool in prioritizing the competitiveness agenda. The industrial sector growth and diversification agenda has moved toward pragmatic, evidence-based, and market-driven processes of problem solving through public-private partnerships. This approach to competitiveness recognizes the processes through which successful industries have emerged, particularly in East Asia. Whether an initial set of competing firms becomes a competitive industry depends both on firm-specific factors as well as on an "ecosystem" of public and quasipublic goods outside the firm. Promising sectors that are new to a country or region inevitably place new demands on the investment climate in terms of regulation, infrastructure, standards, skills, or finance.

As the industry moves toward the competitive frontier, more specialized demands emerge and require solutions. In this view, building competitiveness is essentially a search for technological, policy, institutional, and financial solutions to problems facing an industry at each successive stage of its growth. The experience of newly industrialized countries suggests that this problem-solving process is often led by public-private partnerships.

Correcting the Antiyouth Bias

Young people's labor market prospects have suffered greatly from the antiyouth bias of the structural adjustment period. The youth-led uprisings of the Arab Spring provide a unique opportunity to adopt more youth-friendly labor market policies. The policy framework must strive to increase access to formal jobs with social protection without reverting back to creating unproductive public employment or overly rigid labor market rules. In the long run, this will depend on the adoption of policies that boost labor demand through a healthy investment climate and rapid growth and that improve the quality and composition of the labor supply through stronger, more responsive education systems. However, there are a number of short-run interventions that can make labor markets more hospitable to youth. Active labor market policies, such as job search assistance, employability training support for apprenticeship and internship programs, and on-the-job training subsidies are needed to ease the transition of youth into formal employment.

Governments have traditionally spent significant resources on vocational training for new entrants, but these resources have generally been wasted because they did not cater to the needs of private employers. Public sector training centers that supply most of the training simply have no mechanism to respond to market needs. What is needed is a more market-oriented approach to training that allows employers to shape the kind of training they need with financial support from the government. This can be done through the use of training vouchers that can be redeemed with accredited private sector training providers or through industry-led training centers such as the Penang Skills Development Center (PSDC) in Malaysia. PSDC is a nonprofit, industry-governed training center started in 1989, which serves the needs of the Penang manufacturing industry on the basis of a tripartite partnership between industry, academia, and government. The key to such training institutions is responsiveness to the training needs of private employers, including SMEs.

Finally, the avoidance of the high rates of informality that characterize many labor markets in the Arab world will depend on choosing institutional arrangements that do not impose excessive costs on employers who hire workers formally. These include regulations that set minimum wages, determine social insurance contributions, and protect job security. As Santiago Levy argues in his book on Mexico—*Good Intentions, Bad Outcomes*—when access to social benefits is linked to an individual's labor status, salaried or nonsalaried, and is paid for by wage-based contributions from workers and employers, there is a tendency to push both workers and firms into informality.[14] He further argues that informality is not innocuous, but that it imposes social costs, especially on workers who are excluded from formality, as well as economic costs, in the form of lower labor and capital productivity and, ultimately, lower growth. He proposes a system of universal social entitlements financed from general tax revenues that delinks much of social protection from job status. Because of the high costs of formality, the slowdown in public hiring in Arab economies in recent years has simply translated into an explosion of informality, especially among the growing number of young educated new entrants.

Private Provision of Public Services

Significant improvement of the quality and the productivity of government services could be made by using new technologies as well as providing the legal and incentive framework for the effective private delivery of some services. In the short and medium run, there is a need to improve the quality of the people working in the public sector and to maximize the use of new technologies, including information and communication technology (ICT) in order to enhance service delivery.

Human resources are the main pillar for effective and efficient government service delivery. They should be well qualified, carefully selected, well trained, well managed, and their performance should be continuously evaluated. In this regard, there is a need for attracting better quality civil servants to the public sector by targeting good candidates from schools and universities, offering good salary and remuneration packages, and improving the selection

---

14 Santiago Levy, (2008), *Good Intentions, Bad Outcomes: Social Policy, Informality, and Economic Growth in Mexico* (Washington, DC: Brookings Institution Press).

criteria for candidates. This should be followed by continuous on-the-job training. It is equally important to retain the existing qualified employees by continuously motivating them, including through the improvement of the salary structure and the remuneration package. Moreover, a career path linked with performance should be established for each employee where the career path is based on commitment and accountability.

In parallel, the adoption of different approaches to service delivery, including leaner processes and the greater use of ICT, will tremendously enhance the efficiency of government services. The government should aim to align its business processes and operations with the infrastructure of ICT, which should lead to the integration of all government services across agencies. Also, the use of electronic government services (e-government) will improve the way government extends services to businesses and the public.

Outtasking/outsourcing noncore tasks in government ministries and institutions would have significant advantages in terms of quality and productivity, which, in turn, would create opportunities for new, successful private industries to emerge in service delivery functions. The government could start by pooling services together under one entity and then privatizing it. A good example would be to pool the information technology services in government institutions and allow the private sector to provide the support through service level agreements. This would be efficient and have the side benefit of freeing government institutions to focus on their core tasks of policymaking, regulation, funding, and client service provision.

To reduce the risks of outsourcing, government should start the process gradually, focusing on areas where the services could be successfully handled by the private sector. As an example, government hospitals could start outsourcing their food, cleaning, and engineering services and IT management. It is also important to manage staff movements carefully and effectively in the outsourced areas and to provide training and placement for employees who lose their original positions.

The agenda described demands a repositioning of the relationship between public and private actors, with private actors called on to deliver public goods. Beyond this, the agenda demands judicious risk taking. Such risk taking is best undertaken when supported by rigorous impact measurement and evaluation, so as to support self-correction and adjustment.

STRATEGIC CHOICES IN PRIVATE SECTOR REFORM

Governments around the world pursue a variant of two broad strategies for private sector reform: broad-based, bottom-up strategies or a more focused effort built around strategic initiatives or industries, commonly referred to as industrial policy. In practice, elements of each approach will form the basis of policy, but choices will need to be made in each case. A third strategy, somewhat of a hybrid, would be to focus on creating an environment for high potential entrepreneurs, including social entrepreneurs, to emerge.

Broad-Based Strategies: Empowering Markets

A broad-based strategy to private sector reform should focus on making markets work more effectively by introducing modern tools of regulation in place of outdated administrative controls. Not simple liberalization, it should be construed as a pragmatic approach to efficient private sector development.

If administrative choices and public policy were perfectly and continuously aligned with the most productive use of skilled labor, land, and capital, then there would be no problem. But one of the key reasons that countries have moved away from the administrative control of markets is that markets are dynamic and internalize information. Administrative tools can simply not keep up with the rapid evolution of markets and opportunities. That is one reason why there is such a large stock of obsolete regulation, as in the case of Egypt and Tunisia, and such a gross mismatch between the stock of educated graduates in Tunisia and the market for their skills.

This requires a rethinking of regulation. Regulation in far too many instances is failing to deliver intended benefits, while also imposing high costs. However, simple deregulation is clearly not the answer. Market failures exist, and citizens are right to demand that the private sector adheres to clearly defined public norms. If the question is the balance between public and private interests, a key instrument to remedy this is better business regulation. Good regulation protects the public interest—such as a safe environment, safe food, fair competition, and the prevention of unmanaged risks—but allows good firms to thrive. Good regulations are predictable, efficient, and fair. Some of the characteristics of better regulation:

- *Participatory.* Good regulation emerges from a well-structured dialogue with the private sector, through which public interests can be more clearly specified and regulatory failures—overlaps, unclear provisions, high costs—can be identified. Beyond dialogue, the private sector can play a role in enforcement through voluntary standards or self-regulation. Self-regulation can help achieve objectives efficiently and can be enforced through a threat to use formal state regulation if industry does not deliver. New Zealand has allowed industry to come up with voluntary standards for reducing carbon dioxide emissions, but if this fails, New Zealand will introduce a carbon tax.

- *Differentiated.* A good example of differentiated regulation is border control, where there is a clear public interest in preventing illegal or dangerous goods from entering the country. Countries that regulate borders badly tend to inspect every container, creating delays, damage, and a strong incentive for importers to pay bribes. The government of Morocco used information technology to identify those shipments that create the most risk and inspects only 5 to 10 percent of shipments. The rate of detection of bad shipments increased. The public interest is better protected, trade is faster, and firms are more competitive.

- *Efficient.* Like many countries, the government of Tunisia had reformed many laws and regulations, but often it did not remove the old regulations. Based on a decree of the prime minister of Tunisia, the Ministry of Finance has now created a high-level technical committee and working groups in all departments to look at 500 formalities and eliminate those that are unnecessary, ineffective, not based on law, or redundant. The task will be completed by March, creating a much more competitive environment for its own recovery as the new Tunisia.

- *Predictable.* Private firms, whether individual entrepreneurial entities or large corporate entities, exist to earn a profit commensurate with the risk of investment undertaken. The lack of predictability of the regulatory environment is at least as important to investors as its cost.

- *Accountable.* Oversight by elected legislatures and legislative development based on hearings and stakeholder input will increase the legitimacy of legal rulings. As laws become more important, this will help limit administrative discretion so as to provide increasing clarity and predictability to the private sector as to how the rules will be applied to firms.

Democratizing access to credit will involve building institutions (including credit bureaus), secured lending regimes, and oversight capacity that will allow for the merit-based allocation of capital, rather than allocation based on the presence of collateral or policy preferences.

Building confidence in the judiciary to uphold property rights, even in light of pressure from politically connected interests, is a central challenge of the postrevolution investment climate. Confidence has actually increased over time in several countries of the region, yet the courts remain fundamentally backlogged and inefficient. Judges are not provided with adequate resources, including court staff, court reporting, and clerks for research and administrative functions, and economic training. To help diversify the economy, a few key areas of law are crucial. Strengthening the insolvency and secured transactions systems will encourage risk taking as it allows a debtor to emerge fairly from a failed venture with the ability to learn and leverage the experience into a new venture.

Enhancing competition should be a focus for key sectors across the region. A broad-based strategy to private sector reform would be based on a vision of individual firms making choices that raise their productivity, driven by the process of competition. From a business standpoint, the goal would be to lower the fixed costs of entry and operation, allow unit costs of key inputs to reflect their economic value, while expanding opportunities for growth.

Competition policy provides a partial answer. Egypt has a good Competition Authority, but its effectiveness has been limited due to many exceptions to its mandate. The law and executive regulations could be amended to allow it to cover mergers and acquisitions, and its autonomy could be enhanced by removing the minister of trade from decision making and enforcement processes. Administrative enforcement of the competition authority's rulings could be allowed, and its investigatory powers and ability to impose penalties could be strengthened. Finally, the competition authorities should be supported in a sector-by-sector review to identify barriers to entry, exit, and competition in key sectors, including public utilities.

This is a broad agenda, but the potential benefits are enormous. The evidence is that there are more than 20 million small enterprises in the region, so any marginal improvement in productivity through a broad-based reform could quickly result in significant increases in output and employment.

Scaling up Entrepreneurship—Commercial and Social

Getting the investment climate right for all firms is a long-term agenda. A narrower strategy might productively focus on what Dan Isenberg calls the "entrepreneurship ecosystem"—the combination of culture, infrastructure, policies, regulations, skills, technologies, and capital that are specific to enabling startups to emerge and thrive. The precise formula must be local and cannot be forced into existence, but a wealth of international experience can be applied as guiding principles for the region.[15] Several parts of the broader agenda, particularly around the decriminalization of business failure, streamlining the overwhelming burden of administrative controls and democratizing access to credit, are essential.

The entrepreneurial nature of the revolutions in the region gives confidence that there are relevant skills among youth to be tapped. Building on the success of the revolution may help address the largest challenge, which is cultural: getting young students to see entrepreneurship as a viable choice. Here Injaz's annual Young

15 Danial J. Isenberg, (2010), "How to Start an Entrepreneurial Revolution," *Harvard Business Review*, available at http://hbr.org/2010/06/the-big-idea-how-tostart- an-entrepreneurial-revolution/ar/1.

Entrepreneurs Competition, building on national competitions among schools, is playing an important role in raising the profile and skills required. Efforts to promote mentorship such as Endeavor are also important.

Finally, there is a role for the strategic deployment of capital through investment funds with the capability to identify and accelerate entrepreneurship and private sector development in the region. With a few important exceptions, such as Abraaj's Riyada Enterprise Development Fund, Silatech, and the incubator arms of several of the region's private equity funds, the availability of growth capital for capable smaller firms is as limited as debt, particularly beyond the IT sector. Given the substantial available capital in the region, raising funds should be a less binding constraint than ensuring venture capitalist (VC) talent for identifying and supporting capable firms as well as improving their governance. The latter is likely to require the return of private equity talent from global markets to support the emergence of the Middle East and North Africa region.

Many young entrepreneurs are now focused on enterprise development with a social, rather than financial, impact. They are applying the power of markets to create enterprises that apply commercial principles but through reducing costs are able to provide services to poor consumers or address social issues such as recycling, low-cost housing, education, microfinance, small renewable energy, animal husbandry, and consumer goods. Many of these enterprises originate from the NGO sector but face tremendous hurdles in registration, access to finance, and operations, in part because they operate on narrow margins and in part because there are no legal options for hybrid social enterprises. Removing those obstacles can help the private sector reestablish a "social license" to operate, while also creating sustainable sources of job creation for many inspired youth.

Focused, Strategic Initiatives

Governments cannot do everything, and there is some justification for focused, strategic initiatives through which public action can crowd in the private sector, especially in countries where diversification is a key issue. The broad academic consensus is that diversification requires a combination of supportive exchange rate policy that promotes tradable sectors along with industrial policies.[16] The region appears to be inclined toward active industrial policy. Most countries have spent huge sums on commissioned reports by the world's most reputable consulting firms advising them on the growth of sectors and industries. In Jordan, each sector has been studied multiple times. Lebanon has had 13 sectors studied in depth. Morocco and Libya each recently completed engagements covering industries and sectors. Saudi Arabia has launched programs to build economic centers, an initiative to improve competitiveness (the "10x10" program), and other ambitious efforts. The role models for this approach would be Korea, Singapore, and Malaysia in East Asia and Dubai within the region.

Yet this inventory of studies has produced few clear successes. The reasons for the low success rate are largely the same as the reasons for a failure to sustain broad-based reform: the lack of government implementation capacity and the lack of evaluation. Strategic initiatives are even more demanding of the public sector in ensuring horizontal and vertical coordination, sustained effort, and the avoidance of capture. In the best examples, focused initiatives are highly selective and either reversible or executed on a "no regrets" basis by targeting areas that have broad benefits to society.

16 Dani Rodrik, (2007), "Industrial Development: Stylized Facts and Policies" in UN Department of Economic and Social Affairs, *Industrial Development for the 21st Century* (New York: UN-DESA).

What areas might be most relevant? Several sectors appear to have had a good deal of traction recently, including ICT, tourism, logistics, and the education sector. Internet usage in Arab countries rose 39 percent in 2010, to 86 million people. Leading companies (Intel and Microsoft) have been attracted to Egypt as an outsourcing center, and these services now generate more than $1.1billion in revenue and employ 65,000 workers. There is similarly high potential for Jordan (serving the GCC) and Morocco (serving the European Union [EU]). For many countries, e-government has been a catalyst. Egypt is not exploiting Suez as a logistics corridor, and Libya has not started to tap its tourism potential.

The challenge for such strategic initiatives is how the tools of the state should be deployed. There is a broad consensus that government efforts should be temporary, evaluated and quickly ended if they are not yielding results. They should be neutral to the type of industry that will benefit to the extent possible (or favor sectors with a broad, rather than narrow, impact).[17] Moreover, modern industrial policy is better understood as a process of joint learning and problem solving between the public and private sector, in which the next policy or action in a sequence is not understood until a first step is taken. It is not about the state picking activities and subsidizing them to create industries. This formulation requires that policy makers engage in an ongoing conversation with the private sector to prioritize such actions as the removal of constraints that arise in the diversification process, such as logistics problems, information gaps, or poorly designed institutions.[18] In that conversation, the existence of a state-owned enterprise can even be beneficial and a

17 Commission on Growth and Development, (2008), *Growth Report: Strategies for Sustained Growth and Inclusive Development.*

18 Charles F. Sabel, (2007), "Bootstrapping Development: Rethinking the Role of Public Intervention in Promoting Growth," in Nee and Swedberg, eds, *On Capitalism* (Palo Alto, CA: Stanford University Press), p. 305.

source of information that helps avoid policy capture by the private sector, as long as the enterprise is efficiently run. This illustrates the complexity of simplistic strategies and the need for pragmatism in developing industrial policies.

For any strategy that depends on public investment or intervention, monitoring and evaluation are essential. Diversification is a strategy that calls for self-discovery, so evaluation is of high importance. Evaluation can be technically complex or simple, but it is important that it be undertaken in order to both support and terminate activities based on their success in achieving strategic goals. Where feasible, public interventions should be piloted, in a manner that allows for evaluation using experimental or quasiexperimental methods, to maximize learning.

Chapter 6

NEW REGIONAL AND GLOBAL STRATEGIES

In tandem with the new nationalism of Arab politics, there is a need for a more constructive engagement with the rest of the world. Many countries in the region have favorable access to markets but have not leveraged these opportunities. The region has lost global market share in many export sectors, and nonoil exports represent less than 1 percent of world trade, which is the lowest share of any region. That is not because Arab economies would not benefit from greater international integration. As in other parts of the world, when Arab countries have opened their economies, it has resulted in improved efficiency and productivity growth.[1]

In the current context, there are three reasons why Arab countries should seriously develop coherent strategies toward the rest of the world. First, openness is a major potential source of competition to ensure that the domestic private sector becomes more efficient and grows in a sustainable way. Second, when openness is cemented through international agreements and understandings, it can provide a lock-in for reforms and a mechanism to enhance the long-run credibility of change. There are various levels of such lock-ins, from those that involve treaty obligations such as the World

---

1 Mary Hallward-Driemeier and Fraser Thompson, (2009), "Creative Destruction And Policy Reforms," Policy Research Working Paper 5085, Washington, DC, for a case study on Morocco's trade reforms in the 1990s.

Trade Organization to the norms and expectations contained in letters of understanding to other public policy commitments made to international organizations. Third, openness can help attract the financial and other resources needed to reduce the transition costs of economic reform and to avert short-term crises.

Openness can be pursued simultaneously at the regional and global level. Globally, the key issue is access to markets, while regionally the key issue is the ability to drive down the transaction costs of trade, by addressing nontariff barriers and harmonizing policies. Both are important for Arab economies. Global markets offer the greatest potential opportunities. Regional markets are likely to remain limited, because of the lack of complementarity in production and trade structures across the region, but still present untapped possibilities that might be easier to exploit with simple policy change. Evidence suggests that the match between desired imports and available exports within the region is generally poor and remains significantly below the level found in successful regional communities.

Other impediments to regional integration are a result of policy choices and consist of uneven levels of import protection (widely dispersed tariff rates), high levels of nontariff barriers, and poor logistics (involving customs, port, and transport arrangements). While most trade agreements focus on reciprocal tariff reductions, the removal of nontariff barriers and the improvement of logistics would provide greater welfare benefits at this stage.

In addition to leaving several Arab countries uncertain about their future, recent events in the region have also thrown the regional strategies of international organizations and governments into doubt. Arab countries have traditionally been dealt with in a common fashion, but this now belies a significant amount of variation across countries in the region in terms of a number of characteristics. This regional diversity, combined with the likelihood that the Arab Spring has affected countries unevenly, suggests that it is time to develop a new set of regional and global strategies.

INTEGRATING WITH THE REGION AND THE WORLD

Economic and political integration efforts have a long history in the Arab region but a checkered track record. A large number of preferential trade agreements have been signed in the past five decades, leading to an intertwined and overlapping network of regional organizations. Every Arab country is a party to at least one regional economic agreement, and many countries are members of five or more. Many bilateral investment and cooperation agreements among Arab states add further to the complicated web of regional arrangements.

There is little reason to expect deeper Arab economic integration in the short to medium run, as there is little likelihood that Arab countries would give up sovereignty and form a union. A union would imply redistribution and the politics in the region would not favor that. Institutions such as the Arab League require parallel structures, equivalent to the European Commission and European Parliament, in order to be effective. At the moment the Arab world does not have these institutions, but as the process of democratization goes on that could change and lead to a new wave of regional integration. The key will be the willingness of regional economies to share information, which is the central pillar both of modern border control and modern commerce.

For the time being, despite all efforts, the promise of regional integration has remained largely unrealized. At present, intraregional exports are about 9 percent of all merchandise exports and about 25 percent of all nonoil merchandise exports, lower than in all other regions of the world, except for South Asia. Gravity models that estimate trade potential between partner countries based on economic size, geographical distance, and other country characteristics consistently find that trade among regional economies in the Arab world is below the levels predicted.

Intraregional Trade

As Figure 6.1 shows, intraregional trade remains a fraction of total trade among Arab nations (for whom trade in oil and gas represents approximately half of all trade). Beginning in 2000, due to some renewal of preferential schemes among the Arab nations, the aggregate regional trade volume began to increase. Where regional agreements have succeeded in promoting intraregional trade, there are strong complementarities between the export baskets of some member countries and the import baskets of others. Arab nations are generally more complementary with their advanced country trading partners (the EU and the United States) than with their neighbors within the region.

One way of measuring the potential for regional integration is by calculating the bilateral complementarity index between countries in the region, a measure that compares the similarity between the product mix in one country's export basket and another country's import basket. When the two are identical, the index takes a value of 100. When a country does not export any goods that the partner imports, the index takes a value of zero. Complementarity indexes between partners in successful regional agreements, such as the EU or the North American Free Trade Agreement (NAFTA), exceed 50. The bilateral complementarity between most Arab countries is low; the index generally has single-digit values. Not surprisingly, the complementarity of nonoil trade is higher than for total trade, but nonoil complementarity indices between Arab countries still

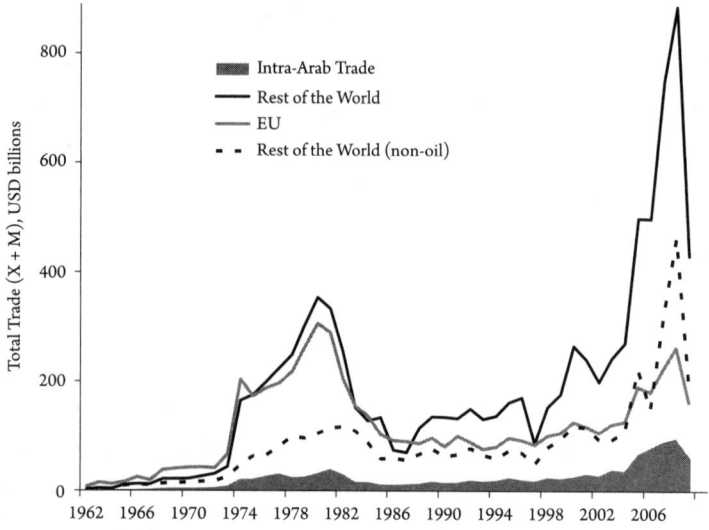

Figure 6.1. Arab Trade. This graph shows total imports and exports of 16 Arab states with different partner groups in constant 2010 dollars. US dollars are deflated by US CPI. Non-oil and gas trade excludes SITC (rev. 1) 33 and 34. (*Source:* UN Commodity Trade Statistics database, http://comtrade.un.org, 2011.)

rarely exceed 20. Only Lebanon and Syria send more than half of their nonoil exports to regional markets. The regional market share is in the single digits for Morocco, Tunisia, Algeria, and Libya.[2]

Within the region, GCC countries have made substantial progress toward a customs union, a common value added tax (VAT), legislative alignment, and even a common currency (although the latter issue will require the resolution of certain intra-GCC disputes over surveillance). By contrast, arrangements in the Maghreb, or the Greater Arab Free Trade Area, have moved slowly. Far more can be done to expand market access and reduce nontariff barriers to trade: examples include the harmonization of customs regulations and practice (regional and international), the mutual recognition of quality standards, and joint border clearance.

2 Mustapha Kemal Nabli, (2007), *Breaking the Barriers to Higher Economic Growth: Better Governance and Deeper Reforms in the Middle East and North Africa* (Washington DC: World Bank).

Finding Regional and Global Markets

The low ratio of nonenergy exports to GDP among countries in the Arab region is among the clearest signs of a lack of global competitiveness and indicates that a potential source of job creation has not been tapped. There are possible complementarities and efficiency gains to be had in the region based on trade integration, including through a more specialized distribution of agricultural investment, economies of scale in some manufactures, and positioning the region as a trade hub between Asia, Africa, and Europe. A few countries, such as Morocco and Tunisia, have made tangible steps in penetrating the European market, but as a whole the region is far below its potential.

The proliferation of Arab regional agreements, however, has hindered integration. Unlocking regional trade will require focusing on institutions that support regional markets by reducing cross-border transaction costs. The range of overlapping trade agreements, including Aghadir, the Common Market for Eastern and Southern Africa (COMESA), Greater Arab Free Trade Area (GAFTA), Mediterranean initiatives, and World Trade Organization (WTO) accession for a number of countries in the region make it clear that tariffs are unlikely to explain the lack of regional trade.

Different regional initiatives have different sector and product coverage, different liberalization schedules, and different rules of origin. Implementation agencies, such as customs, often lack the capacity to put the agreement provisions into practice. The first order of business in creating effective regional integration is therefore to rationalize and streamline existing agreements to eliminate overlapping and conflicting rules and administrative procedures.

Despite the substantial number of formal regional agreements to liberalize trade, moreover, there is an unfinished agenda of border reforms that need to be implemented. The Arab-wide average tariff has been tending toward the world average. However, the spread in average tariff rates among Arab countries remains substantial, and countries with relatively high duties on average are vulnerable to trade diversion.

In many cases, nontariff barriers significantly offset the trade preferences embodied in regional agreements. Nontariff barriers to trade are more substantial in the Arab region than in any other region of the world, and they contribute more to overall trade restrictiveness than tariffs. Firm surveys suggest that the cost of complying with nontariff barriers is more than 10 percent of the value of goods shipped. Nontariff barriers are particularly pervasive and restrictive in labor-abundant Arab countries. They are far less restrictive in the resource-rich, labor-importing countries of the region.

Several Arab countries, including Egypt, Morocco, and Tunisia, have undertaken unilateral trade reforms. In 2004, Egypt cut tariffs, reduced its number of tariff bands from 25 to 6 and its number of tariff lines from 13,000 to 6,000. The result was a significant reduction in the weighted mean tariff. Egypt is now more open to trade than the average country in the region. Still, like the majority of other countries in the region, Egypt is more protective of its agricultural goods (with a trade restrictiveness index of 7 percent) than its nonagricultural goods (5.4 percent).

Trade procedures are relatively more difficult and time consuming to undertake in Arab countries than in other middle-income economies. Although Arab governments require lighter importing and exporting documentation, on average, than their counterparts in low-income sub-Saharan Africa or in South Asia, the number of documents substantially exceeds the averages for middle-income Latin American and East Asian economies.

Beyond tariffs, behind-the-border issues need to be addressed. Egypt's Logistics Performance Index score for 2010, which reflects the extent of its trade facilitation, is below the regional and income group averages. Egypt scores 2.37 on a scale of 1 to 5, with 5 being the highest score, slightly below the regional and income group averages of 2.42 and 2.47, respectively. It ranked ninety-seventh out of 150 ranked countries and sixth in the Arab region. One reason is that the "container" revolution has not reached Egypt. Its legal and regulatory framework does not recognize containers inland, nor intermodal transport.

Poor trade logistics also play a significant role in raising trade friction costs, in general, and in restricting intraregional trade. Most Arab countries score below the level of logistics performance that would be predicted from their level of income (see Figure 6.2). The most marked logistics challenges are observed in the resource-rich, labor-abundant countries that have pronounced gaps in logistics competence and cargo tracking and tracing.

Services, Workers, and Investment

Existing agreements in the Arab world generally do not cover trade in services. Where they do, provisions are vague and refer only to

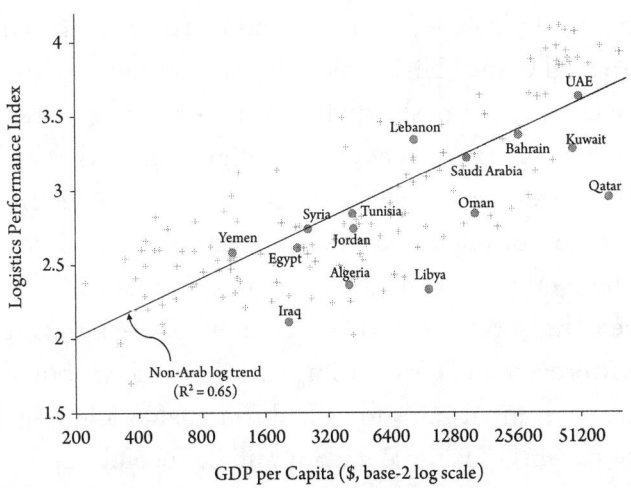

Figure 6.2. Income and Trade Logistics Performance, 2009. (*Source:* World Bank. *World Development Indicators,* http://data.worldbankorg/indicator, 2009.)

"intentions to cooperate" in certain services sectors. Intraregional differences in regulations, restrictions on currency convertibility, and limits on the physical movement of individuals have created a situation in which it is often easier for Arab-country service providers to operate outside the region, such as in Europe, than within it.

In services, as in trade in goods, making regional agreements consistent with other preferential trade agreements can expand trade in the services sector and would be an important step toward increasing firm capabilities and competitiveness. Those Arab countries that have concluded free trade agreements with the United States and the European Union have included services sector provisions—notably banking, insurance, and telecommunications—in the agreements. But the current arrangements generally simply lock in existing rules with respect to openness to services providers. Only a few cases, such as the banking sector in Bahrain, have involved changes in restricted activities.

Arab labor markets, on the other hand, are among the most integrated in the world, yet migration policy is conducted wholly on a country-by-country basis. Extending regional agreements to define the rights and obligations of migrant workers and to spell out codes of conduct for host countries would be a major step toward assuring greater transparency in the migration market and reducing the scope for political shocks to migration and remittance flows. Formalization of migration rules in a multilateral context would benefit both migrants and host country governments.

Given the surplus of skilled labor in labor-abundant Egypt, Jordan, Morocco, and the large imports of skilled labor in the GCC, there are substantial gains to be had from better aligning the skill delivery systems of labor-abundant middle-income countries with the needs of labor-importing markets, and from facilitating the flow of such labor. Simple measures can go a long way, for example, common regional visas for professionals (ICT, engineering, consulting, finance) or ICT-based solutions to allow easier access to major technology procurements.

The oil boom of the 1970s led to an explosive growth of migration from labor-abundant economies in North Africa into the GCC countries, but as oil prices fell in the mid-1980s, labor demand fell, and Arab migrant workers faced increased competition at both ends of the skills spectrum. At the high end, GCC countries restricted access by foreigners to public administration jobs and put pressure on the private sector to hire nationals. At the unskilled end, Arab workers were replaced by South and Southeast Asian workers, because of their willingness to work for lower wages and in poorer working conditions. Asian migrants moved without families, an implicit guarantee of voluntary return, making them more attractive workers for host countries.

National preference policies, competition from Asian workers, and political tensions resulted in a leveling off of intraregional labor flows in the 1990s. Today, intra-Arab migration stands at approximately 4.5 million migrants, mostly in the GCC. This number exceeds the number of Arab migrants living in Europe. Arab migrants are overwhelmingly living in other Arab countries.

Finally, intraregional foreign direct investment (FDI) and portfolio investment have risen with oil prices. The booming oil revenues accruing to the GCC countries have been partly recycled within the region. Between 2002 and 2006, about $60 billion, or 11 percent of total GCC capital outflows, went to other Arab countries. Compared with previous oil booms, a higher amount of the surplus available to the oil-exporting Arab countries is being channeled into project-based investments in the region. GCC countries have allocated more than $1.3 trillion to infrastructure and manufacturing investments in the region over the next five years. The GCC sovereign wealth funds are increasingly looking for opportunities in

Arab states, both because of the perceived potential in Arab markets and the de facto restrictions the funds face in OECD economies.

Linking Regional and Global Agreements

In East Asia and other parts of the world, trade agreements have been used to cement domestic reform programs in place; it is difficult for antireform groups to force reversals on governments once international agreements are made, since doing so would require consent by all regional partner countries. This role of enhancing policy credibility is particularly important for services and investment reforms, which often aim to attract large-scale, long-term investors to the country. In a period of rapid change, regional standards and codes of good practice can also strengthen public scrutiny of policy makers,[3] and they can provide a basis for replication.

Recently agreements with partners from outside the region, notably the European Union and the United States, have assumed a prominent role. Examples include the Euro-Mediterranean Agreements of the European Union with several Mediterranean-Arab countries, as well as the bilateral agreements between the United States and Bahrain, Jordan, Lebanon, Morocco, and Oman. Both the Euro-Med agreements and the country-by-country preferential trade agreements with the United States are "hub and spoke" arrangements that do not encourage the development of regional value chains. Intraregional rules of origin are markedly different from those in the Euro-Mediterranean agreements, so that companies wanting to serve both Arab and European markets have to run parallel procurement and production processes to satisfy their respective requirements. In the medium term, it will be important

---

3 Paul Collier, (2010), *Plundered Planet* (Oxford: Oxford University Press).

to harmonize the European and American preferential agreements and make them compatible with regional agreements.

Unfortunately, most regional agreements in the Arab world look stronger on paper than in practice. There is often a lack of trust and commitment—for example, in the discretionary application of administrative rules and requirements—that hampers proper implementation. Well-functioning monitoring mechanisms and sustained high-level political attention to institutional improvements, such as those concerning reductions in tariff and nontariff barriers, are essential for the success of regional integration initiatives. Technical reviews of progress toward the agreements' objectives should be undertaken on a regular basis, and senior officials need to act on the recommendations of these reviews.

REGIONAL INFRASTRUCTURE COOPERATION

In 1914, the Hejaz Railway ran more than 800 miles from the Levant to the Arabian Peninsula, carrying freight and passengers from Damascus to Medina. But four years later the railway was famously destroyed in the Arab revolt against Ottoman armies led by Lawrence of Arabia. Despite proclamations from Arab states to the contrary, the railway was never rebuilt.

The lack of rail transport in the Arab world underscores the problems of cooperation in the region: political animosities, a diversity of standards, and a lack of economic incentive to cooperate. Rail lines in Morocco stop abruptly at the Algerian border. Jordan has only narrow-gauge rail. Despite crushing amounts of road traffic in the booming cities of the GCC, only Saudi Arabia has an operating passenger and freight rail system—connecting Riyadh to the port city of Damman. Less than 10 percent of track in the Arab region is double track, and less than 3 percent is electrified. Prior to the Arab Spring, several Arab countries had drawn up plans for ambitious rail projects. Qatar and Kuwait were to spend around $10 billion each, the United Arab Emirates $20 billion, and Saudi Arabia $15 billion. In Saudi Arabia, a high-speed railway along the old Hejaz line to Medina and through to Mecca was planned. More importantly, these national lines were to be connected into a regional network. The financial crisis in Dubai, the global financial crisis, and of course, the events of the Arab Spring appear to have shelved many of these plans.

Revisiting these efforts means facing steep political, regulatory, and financial challenges. As the history of successful regional integration efforts elsewhere has shown, building the governance structures that can support the construction and maintenance of transborder infrastructure is an important confidence-building mechanism for eventual deeper integration. Regional infrastructure projects could do much to help boost regional economies in the short run, during the construction phase, and even more in the long run.

A number of regional infrastructure projects—electricity grids, gas pipelines, and telecommunication networks—also hold promise. An abundance of sunshine, clear skies, desert land, and proximity to Europe, for example, makes North Africa the most globally competitive location for concentrated solar power (CSP).[4] The question is whether international and domestic action can be energized by the political imperative for job creation coming from the Arab Spring movement. Indeed, the G8 in its May 2011 Deauville Summit Declaration on the Arab Spring, encouraged multidonor partnerships for regional integration, with solar power

---

4 Each square kilometer of desert land can harvest up to 250 gigawatt hours of electricity per year with the concentrated solar thermal power plants.

development cited as a priority.[5] The vision of a strong solar industry in the region has been under development for some years, supported by international initiatives and private sector partnerships.[6]

Solar industry could bring benefits to the region as an early entrant to the market, allowing the region to become a center for research and development while attracting entrepreneurs who specialize in providing the necessary equipment and expertise.[7] Most solar components could be manufactured locally. Arab oil importers could also enhance their energy security as well as bring in export earnings by relying on solar electricity. Arab states are a particularly rich source of renewable energy for Europe since the Arab region's high solar resource could compensate for the additional cost of long transmission lines.[8]

5 *Declaration of the G8 on the Arab Springs*, G8 Summit of Deauville, May 27, 2011, http://www.g20-g8.com/g8-g20/g8/english/live/news/declaration-of-the-g8-on-the-arab-springs.1316.html.

6 The Mediterranean Solar Plan (MSP) is a political initiative that is an initiative of the Union of the Mediterranean (UfM), which consists of the heads of states and governments of the European and Mediterranean countries. MSP aims at developing 20 gigawatts of renewable electricity capacity as well as the grid infrastructure for the energy interconnection with Europe by 2020. It has focused on development of grid interconnections among Mediterranean countries and the EU. Desertec is another initiative that focuses on promoting private sector investment for the production of electricity and desalinated water by developing CSP and wind turbines in Middle Eastern and North African deserts.

7 A scenario that provides for the completion of 5 gigawatts by 2020 could yield around 64,000 to 79,000 local jobs by 2025. This would include 46,000 to 60,000 jobs in construction and manufacturing and 19,000 jobs in operation and maintenance. A total of 34,000 employees would permanently work in the solar industry. The IEA envisages that solar power could provide 11 percent of global electricity by 2050, contributing to climate change emission reduction goals. In the sunniest countries and regions, solar power could become a competitive source of bulk power in peak and intermediate loads by 2020, and base load power by 2025 and 2030. IEA, (2010), *Technology Roadmap: Concentrating Solar Power*.

8 Solar investment programs received a boost with the approval in December 2009 of $750 million in highly concessional funding from the Clean Technology Fund that is expected to leverage an additional $4.85 billion from public and private sources. The program aims to cofinance nine commercial-scale power plants with a total capacity of 1.2 gigawatts and two strategic transmission projects in Algeria, Egypt, Jordan, Morocco, and Tunisia. This program's ultimate goal is to trigger further investment from the private

However, solar costs are significantly higher than fossil fuel alternatives (not counting externalities). The cost of electricity produced from the solar plants is between 10 cents per kilowatt hour and 15 cents per kilowatt hour. Electricity produced by conventional coal-fired power plants is as low as 6.2 cents per kilowatt hour. Of course, prices for competing fuels (such as coal and oil) do not account for environmental, health, and other externalities. Moreover, technology-specific barriers—such as the longevity of power-purchase agreements or feed-in-tariff programs and the risks of relying on untried technologies—are significant obstacles. Europe, in particular, has a role in concluding power purchase agreements with tariffs high enough to provide an incentive for the region to invest at sufficient scale to bring down costs and supply enough low-emission energy to help Europe meet its climate goals. Policy risks can be modified by appropriate laws. In recent years, Algeria and Tunisia passed specific renewable energy legislation, and legal frameworks were under development for Egypt and Morocco.

At present, North African power could connect with Europe through the East (via Turkey) or the West (via Spain). But significant areas suitable for solar power generation lie in between, so a well-functioning regional power grid is critical to link generation sites with domestic and international consumption centers. The existing Arab grid is inadequate and requires expansion. Regional initiatives for a common grid remain fragmented, and regional collaboration will require Arab leaders to revive efforts toward energy integration (for example, the GCC's Interconnection Project, which has linked the grids of Kuwait, Saudi Arabia, Bahrain, and Qatar with

---

sector, leading to the installation of more than 5 gigawatts of solar capacity in MENA by 2020. To give a sense of the significance of even these first investments, global solar installed capacity is today about 700 megawatts.

further connections planned for the UAE and Oman) as well as plans for upgrading connections within North Africa.

A ROLE FOR INTERNATIONAL ACTORS?

International actors are viewed with suspicion in many Arab countries. For decades, bilateral donors and international financial institutions ignored problems of social equity, corruption, and a lack of civil society and media freedoms. Any of the effects of renewed attention to government effectiveness and human rights by international actors in recent years have been clouded by their perceived linkages to the highly charged issues of antiterrorism and regional conflict. International actors can play a transformative role in helping countries weather major economic transitions, as they did in eastern European following the collapse of central planning, but their role in the Arab Spring countries remains unclear because of this absence of trust.

It cannot be taken for granted that support from international donors will always be beneficial or welcomed by recipients in the Arab world. In the case of Egypt, the government declined a program loan from the World Bank on the grounds that it was not compatible with its national interest. Some reports suggest the World Bank was trying to attach conditions regarding the passage of a Freedom of Information Act to its support. At the same time, the Egyptian government announced that Saudi Arabia would provide a loan of $200 million to support small and medium enterprises. All this came after Egypt decided not to request an International Monetary Fund (IMF) program after revising and lowering its budgeted deficit target for 2011 and 2012 and deciding to refrain from external borrowing. A recent Gallup poll found that 43 percent of Egyptians were against the idea of accepting any help from the United States, and those sentiments extend to the international financial institutions in which the United States is a significant shareholder.

The context of donor intervention is shaped by these stories. There is no clear pathway toward reform on which the current governments and the international community agree. Given the unique character of the reform process in the Arab world, it would be highly unusual if such a consensus emerged at this early stage. Even within Arab countries, there is unlikely to be full consensus, and new governments and ministers are likely to have their own views on the best way forward. This is quite unlike the transition in eastern Europe when the main path, the desire to create a market economy, was clear to all.

It is also important to bear in mind that there are alternatives to traditional Western donors in the form of the GCC countries. In this, the Arab world transition is quite different from other transitions where there were no alternatives.

The political history of the region constrains many international financial institutions that are perceived in the region as instruments of Western (and more specifically US) foreign policy. Any intervention will inevitably have political ramifications. These cannot be ignored. At the end of the day, crafting a political-economic strategy is needed. The complex politics of the region has already doomed one previous effort at a regional support mechanism. In 1991, a Regional Economic Development Working Group was established as part of the Madrid Peace Conference sponsored by the United States and the Soviet Union. Following that, a number of economic summits on the development of the region were held, leading to the idea of establishing a Middle East Development Bank, as a joint Arab-Israeli institution. In the end, Jordan was the only Arab country to sign the proposed bank charter, the United States could not persuade Congress to fund it, and the initiative died.

Looking to the future, donor intervention in the region can be broken down into three elements: (1) a resource transfer function; (2) an anchor for reforms or alternatively a mechanism for the authorities to precommit to a certain reform path, providing hopefully expectations of a robust intertemporal time consistency; and (3) new ideas for reform strategies that come from other countries and experiences.

The Financing Gap

Most of the Arab countries have substantial fiscal deficits forecast for 2011, ranging from 8.4 percent of the GDP of Egypt (where external debt is topping 75 percent of GDP), Jordan 6.7 (62 percent), Morocco, 4.8 (53 percent), and Tunisia 4.3 (43 percent). As the figures in parentheses show, these deficits are juxtaposed against already sizeable external debt-to-GDP ratios, with Egypt having both the largest deficit and the largest stock of debt. In all cases, actions are contemplated to reduce deficits and to stabilize the debt, but the actual changes in debt ratios will depend on the growth performance of the economies, something that remains uncertain. In all cases, fiscal deficits are dominated by large transfer and subsidy programs that exceed the size of the deficit. That is, all financing of the deficit is, on the margin, going into consumption not investment.

In this context, the preferred financing solution would be to look for grants. However, grants appear to be limited. The G8, while announcing significant support for Egypt, Tunisia, Morocco, and Jordan of $40 billion, (10 percent of the roughly $400 billion nominal GDP of these four countries), only has a small fraction in the form of grants.[9] The rest is in debt, albeit at prevailing low market

9 Libya has also been invited to join the so-called Deauville Partnership.

rates. This complicates the financing pattern and implies that the transition must happen reasonably fast. It would not be tenable, for example, for any of these countries (with the possible exception of Tunisia) to continue to borrow heavily over a three-to-four-year period. The picture may be even worse than depicted here if any of the countries face contingent liabilities from their banking sector, a common phenomenon in economic transitions as banks inevitably suffer large capital losses due to the needed economic restructuring and the costs of the downturns associated with political turmoil. The issue for most Arab countries, therefore, is largely about the timing and sequencing of reforms needed for deficit reduction.

Another way of generating resource transfers in the region is by trying to improve the climate for private financial flows. This can be done by reducing the risk premium on government debt (for example, the United States has just announced its intentions to provide Egypt with $1 billion of debt relief) or by improving the climate for foreign direct investment. In selected cases, carefully targeted guarantees can also help facilitate specific types of project finance.

The balance between short-term deficit financing through grants and credits versus support for other capital flows through policy reforms and guarantees is a key element of any package. International financial institutions have instruments for both purposes.

Reform Commitment

In any major economic transition, uncertainty over the course of future policy is a major problem. Few governments can credibly commit their (unknown) successors to a consistent economic program. The IFIs provide one mechanism for such an intertemporal commitment because their programs are multiyear. This lock-in can be a major advantage. Through their programs, IFIs can also try to instill a sense of urgency of reform and ensure that the scope of reform is adequate to deliver a successful outcome.

To exploit this function to its maximum advantage, it would be useful for government programs to emphasize institutional change. In the Deauville partnership, the IFIs agreed to an economic framework tailored to control corruption, support transparency, and accountability; social and economic inclusion; economic modernization and job creation; the private sector; and regional and global integration. Each of these areas has an important institutional reform component.

In some transition episodes, the anchor for reform commitment has come from other external sources. In the case of eastern European economies, joining the European Union was an important anchor that drove both the scope and pace of reforms. In the Arab world, the proposed Mediterranean Union, built on the existing EU structures and the Barcelona Process and including all EU member states, provides one possible anchor, but it is narrow in scope and slow in program implementation.

The Barcelona Process is designed to build political, economic, and social partnerships between the EU and its southern Mediterranean neighbors. A first step is to create free trade areas, removing most tariff and nontariff barriers, as well as providing for the elimination of investment obstacles and easier flows of technology. Progress has been good in terms of manufacturing, but liberalization of agricultural trade reportedly lags behind. The Euro-Mediterranean countries have also agreed to strengthen civil society and encourage democratic institutions to lead to social development. They would also reduce migration pressures through vocational training and job creation programs.

The key financing arms of the Mediterranean Union are the EU and the European Investment Bank (EIB). But the priority projects, identified prior to the Arab Spring, may need to be adapted to current realities: Depollution of the Mediterranean, improved maritime and land highways, civil protection, alternative energies, higher education and research, and Mediterranean business initiative are important but may need to be supplemented by other programs more critical to the region's needs.

New Ideas

There are a number of potentially relevant experiences faced by other reform programs that the international community can share with Arab countries:

- Guatemala's Historical Clarification Commission is a truth and reconciliation commission that appears to have had some success in helping the country deal with its legacy of political repression and cronyism. It has recently been introduced to Honduras.
- Indonesia's relative success with creating a reputation for aggressively tackling corruption and improving the quality of governance, through the Partnership for Governance Reform and the independent Corruption Eradication Commission (KPK).
- Decentralization, as in Brazil, Colombia, and Indonesia, to put into practice the principle of subsidiarity. Territorial issues are linked to poverty, ethnic concentrations, and border and neighborhood issues. Few Arab countries have significant experience in implementing programs for subregions.
- Experimentation with "charter cities" as a way of jump-starting institutional development in countries faced with major weaknesses in enforcing property rights and

contracts has been proposed and has faced controversy. More modestly, industrial zones and parks can provide an environment with one-stop licensing, good infrastructure, and easy access to a range of desired business services. Service guarantees can even be provided to ensure against possible utility (power, water, transport) outages.

- Guarantee schemes, like the Department for International Development's (DFID's) first-loss financing of housing in Gaza, can attract private capital, leveraging resources for the economic transition.
- Skills programs, like Malaysia's Penang Skills Development Center, that partner government funds in provision of basic infrastructure with private firms' trainers in specific sectoral skills have had great success (but other public job training and vocational training programs have proved very unsuccessful).
- Volunteering programs, like AmeriCorps, can provide immediate opportunities for young, socially dedicated youth.

Next Steps

For the international community to be successful in helping the Arab transition, it must provide all three functions previously discussed in a balanced way. Resources, commitment mechanisms, and innovative programs with a track record of success have to be put on the table. Help is needed both to finance budget deficits in the short term as well as to leverage private finance.

At present, the focus is being placed on existing institutions to provide the needed resources, but new partnerships are also emerging. Proposals have been advanced for an Arab Financing Facility for Infrastructure (AFFI), a Cross-Border Trade Facilitation and Infrastructure Program, and a Joint Approach for Private Sector Development. These ideas suggest it may be time to rethink the idea of an Arab bank that could take the lead in developing and coordinating such programs on behalf of all countries in the region. Such a bank should probably keep its shareholding to regional members, as is common in other regions: The Caribbean, the Andean group, and the Central American Bank for Economic Integration are examples. The advantage of a regional bank is that, thanks to a specific focus, it is dedicated to serving its members. The Central American Bank for Economic Integration (CABEI), for example, provides more resources for infrastructure in the region than the World Bank and the Inter-American Development Bank combined. A regional Arab bank would provide the long-term commitment that is called for. Its governance would bolster economic integration and be free of perceived political interference by the West. It could coexist and partner in professional ways with other institutions. In short, it can provide the kind of institutional base that the region requires.

The history of such regional banks is that they need considerable capital to manage the limited opportunities for diversification that are present, but that overall they can obtain commercial funding at rates that are lower than individual member countries. CABEI, for example, has a 35 percent paid-in capital ratio but compensates by leveraging its capital more than the World Bank, for example.

When it comes to financing, much depends on the exchange rate and the broader orientation of economic policy to promote exports (Box 6.1). So far, the Arab Spring countries have not seen any significant moves in their exchange rates, protecting against depreciation through a variety of measures including capital controls (Tunisia) and the sales of official international reserves (Egypt). It is tempting to try and support the currency to reduce inflationary pressures and keep down the price of imports, especially for

Box 6.1 THE TURKISH EXPERIENCE

Turkey, with its proximity to the Arab countries, as well as the strong historical and cultural ties that span many centuries, is obviously a country that is studied and observed in the Arab world. Turkey's strong engagement with other nations in the region over the last few years has further strengthened economic ties as well as Arab interest in the Turkish experience. Excluding the world recession of late 2008 and 2009, Turkey's recent trend growth rate has been in the 7 to 8 percent range, among the best performers worldwide.

A key feature of the Turkish economy is strong engagement with the outside world and global markets that has led to more rapid productivity growth, scale economies, technological absorption, and product diversification. Yet before the early 1980s, Turkey was a heavily protected and closed economy, with an export-to-GDP ratio of around 5 percent. It then adopted a more export-led strategy, and exports have since climbed to 20 to 25 percent of the GDP. Membership in the European Union's Custom Union in 1996 committed Turkey to an open economy, at least in the industrial sector.

The political economy of this transformation from a closed to a very open economy is interesting. Support to exports came before trade liberalization. Various incentive policies in the 1980s led to good export performance and also to the emergence of a domestic "export lobby" that eventually counteracted strong protectionist interest groups. Many industries transformed themselves from being almost exclusively domestically focused to a clear world market orientation.

continued from previous page

The automotive industry has been a good example of such a transformation and is now highly competitive in the region and the world.

In implementing an outward-looking strategy, Turkey was fortunate in not having to deal with a structural Dutch disease problem, given its absence of natural resource exports. But it did become vulnerable to negative macroeconomic developments in the world economy because it did not successfully support trade reforms with a high national savings rate. The current account of the balance of payments accordingly tends to be in large deficit and exposes the Turkish economy to sudden capital flow reversals.

The Turkish experience, as well as that of many other emerging economies, suggests that there are considerable gains from a strong engagement with world markets. International agreements that establish the credibility of the long-term policy commitment to exports can simultaneously promote long-term capital inflows. But these work best when supported by a sound domestic macroeconomic policy framework, a tax system and macroprudential financial regulations that encourage national savings, a low current account deficit, and a competitive exchange rate that is managed in such a way as to avoid excessive appreciation driven by hot money.

products that the government subsidizes, such as fuel and food. But without allowing the exchange rate to depreciate, the strategies for private sector development and global integration will be jeopardized. Even the public sector reform strategy cannot be adequately assessed as debt dynamics will depend importantly on the future path of the exchange rate.

Private finance, both remittances and foreign investment, is heavily influenced by the exchange rate. At current rates, investment opportunities may be limited given the significant risk involved in the transition in the region. Restoring the risk-reward balance to encourage more private investment is a core function of external assistance.

Limitations of International Organizations

The international community largely works through government-to-government or organization-to-government processes. But when governments and political processes are in transition, there are limits to what external actors can do. Transitional governments typically have a short amount of time to become established, which encourages them to overborrow and delay reform to maximize their popularity. External actors need to support government programs but also have a responsibility to the people. A key lesson from the current unrest is that insufficient attention was paid to the real benefits to the people and that support to governments was extended despite persistent problems of corruption, political repression, and rising socioeconomic inequities. External aid to the region increased at the same time popular dissatisfaction was rising (Figure 6.3). The funds were disbursed following flawed foreign assistance strategies that ignored civil society and these countries' deep-seated shortcomings in governance.

It is now clear that the strategies of many donors and IFIs were based on their own partial and uncritical assessments of country performance. Misgovernance and capture had been endemic throughout the Arab world for a long time, with practically no

Figure 6.3. Evolution of Development Assistance versus Voice and Democratic Accountability in the Arab World, 2000–2009. *Note:* Iraq was excluded because it represents a special case in development assistance given its current situation; it received these amounts of official development assistance from all donors between 2006 and 2008: in 2006, $9.7 billion, of which 52 percent came from the United States; in 2007, $9.7 billion, of which 40 percent came from the United States; and in 2008, $9.8 billion, of which 28 percent came from the United States. WGI = Worldwide Governance Indicators; ODA = official development assistance. (*Source:* D. Kaufmann, A. Kraay, and M. Mastruzzi. *Worldwide Governance Indicators: A Summary of Data, Methodology and Analytical Issues.* Worldwide Governance Indicators Project, 2010, available at www.govindicators.org; Organization for Economic Cooperation and Development, Development Assistance Committee database, www.oecd.org, 2011.)

exceptions. Data pointing to these major political shortcomings were available yet often ignored.

Now that political transitions have started, it is even more important for the international community to make independent assessments of reform progress. Transitions are difficult and unpredictable, and, depending on a number of factors, they can lead a country onto the right path to recovery with better government and sustained, shared growth—or not. Accounting for the initial quality of a country's governance and monitoring its subsequent path, including the challenge of addressing the "informal" institution of capture, is critical. Important challenges in regard to formal institutions during the early stages of the transition, such as multiparty development and constitutional and electoral reform, as well as global security considerations, also should not be under-emphasized. But the latter are already being addressed in a number of writings and are ever present in the media.

The key need is to redefine the role of the international community in the Arab world. Regime change and the rejection of the old, autocratic political order do not automatically guarantee major improvements in the quality of government in the near future; hard work and major reforms will be needed, including new constitutions and competitive elections. The fact that the ruling families, which were at the center of the economic capture network, are out of power does not guarantee a transition away from a captured economy.

Some of the vestiges of the old cronyism may have more stay-ing power and ability to adapt than commonly assumed. The abil-ity of political and economic elites to collect economic rents may not quickly wane and their capital may also flee. In addition, new oligarchs and cronies are likely to emerge during the transition. The military itself may turn out to resist abdicating economic and political power, if its economic interests are threatened, as has hap-pened in other parts of the world.

More generally, these transitions often take place with little transparency and unequal access to information and influence, in settings where checks and balances are still lacking. The Soviet transition offers a more extreme lesson in the oligarchic cap-ture of a vast share of the nation's wealth along with the capture of the legal, regulatory, and policy framework. Yet even for other parts of the world, the challenge of capture is not merely of an aca-demic or moral-ethical nature, and it differs from the traditional call by advocacy NGOs to fight against bureaucratic corruption. Capture matters enormously for the overall economy and its pros-pects. When successful capture is thought to be feasible, there are enormous incentives for talent and resources to be diverted away from competitive productive entrepreneurship and investment.

There is a real but more subtle risk of elite capture during the transition—and this refers to the broader elite, namely, the educated middle to upper class. In Egypt, the majority of the population is still poor and not highly educated or Internet connected, yet such a silent majority has largely been absent in the transition so far. It is also unclear who will represent their interests. The international community must be particularly vigilant to the risk that skewed policymaking will favor the educated elite at the expense of the poor.

Before it can assume its full role, the international community must establish greater trust with the populations of Arab countries. They need to rapidly adapt to the new reality and be prepared to take a humbler role, working to restore their credibility in the aftermath of long years of support for autocratic regimes. They should be respectful of the pace and manner in which progress takes place during the transition and mindful that progress is not always rapid, continuous, or linear. Specifically, in transition countries, they must work closely with civil society groups and other institutions outside the executive branch as well. Their principal modality of focusing on large loans to central governments needs to be revisited, and new instruments for collaboration need to be developed.

In essence, a new "business model" for engagement by the international community is needed, with concrete and detailed pillars. Some organizations—such as the World Bank, International Monetary Fund, and European Union—are already beginning to signal a break from the past and grapple with the need to revamp their strategies. Yet detailed feasible strategies and programs still need to be formulated, and assiduous implementation needs to begin. Considerations of governance should be made much more prominent, focusing on supporting the countries in transition to implement measures that control corruption, enhance transparency, and move away from the risks of economic capture by elites.

The following are concrete suggestions in seven priority areas in the context of such a strategic revamping, which focus on governance and which would also help mitigate the risk of protracted capture:

- *In-depth and neutral assessment of the political challenges in each country.* The international community can find new ways to address the task of country analysis. It will be important that official country reports and analyses by international agencies are carried out with some modicum of independence, written without self-censorship, and cover all important areas for the country's transition, including sensitive political issues such as capture and corruption. These reports may need to be done with support or input from local nongovernmental organizations that are closer to the reality on the ground.

Reports should not shy away from using available data on human rights, corruption, and on the quality of government, and if requested in some cases, consider carrying out in-depth country diagnostics. They should be submitted for external review and scrutiny. Complementing the important role of IFIs, the research and think tank community (possibly in partnership with local and international think tanks or research institutions) can also play a more active role. In this context, an important component is to develop and disseminate more complete and transparent databases and political diagnostics for countries in the region. National-level governance indicators as well as firm-level surveys and in country diagnostics will increasingly need to be factored into responses to the challenges of capture and related nontraditional forms of corruption and misgovernance.

- *Selectivity in aid flows.* The members of the international community need to become more selective in their allocation of aid to the region, paying more attention to governance in the recipient country. Nonreforming governments that do not meet minimum standards in controlling corruption, supporting freedom of speech, and enforcing accountability on political rulers, would not receive aid. This may not preclude supporting reforming institutions and stakeholders outside the executive in countries with entrenched governments.

Yet there should also be improved selectivity in the destination of aid within a country, including carefully selecting partner institutions (again, also including those outside the executive branch) and paying more attention to the subnational level and to competitive private sector development (rather than further strengthening elites). Reforming countries committed to improved governance ought to be supported through an integrated package channeling help to governmental institutions and NGOs alike.

- *Support an integrated package of transparency-led reforms.* To mitigate capture and improve governance, major reforms to reduce information asymmetries and enhance transparency and disclosure must be a priority. Some improvements have started to take place in Egypt and Tunisia, particularly in regard to the Internet and mass media. Drawing from the concrete experiences of other countries, a 10-point program of transparency reforms in the political, economic/financial and institutional arenas could pay off in the countries in transition in the Arab world.[10]

In most economies, including those in transition, a full-fledged level playing field of small- and medium-sized enterprises is unrealistic, at least in the short to medium terms. Hence, the strategy needs to factor in the initial conditions where there are preexisting powerful vested interests, along with some new ones. Within such parameters, a realistic objective would be to mitigate rather than eliminate capture. For this purpose, transparency is crucial, as are a free press and more generally the introduction of competition in the polity through democratic elections and supporting civil society organizations (CSOs).

- *Revamped procurement systems.* A revamped procurement system, with full transparency and competitiveness, is also paramount early in the transition. New technologies, including e-procurement, are important for this dimension of reform, as for supporting many other measures.
- *Supporting the competitive small- and medium-scale private sector.* Agencies dealing with the private sector, such as the International Finance Corporation (the World Bank's private sector affiliate), would also need to become

10 Such a 10-point transparency reform program could include the following: (1) media freedoms, media and internet development; (2) public disclosure of parliamentary debates and votes; (3) effective implementation of conflict of interest laws and the adoption of lobby laws separating business, politics, legislation, and the executive; (4) publicly blacklisting firms bribing in public procurement; (5) adoption and effective implementation of a freedom of information law, with easy access to all to government information; (6) adopting transparency standards for socioeconomic and financial data, including poverty data and fiscal/budget transparency standards; (7) e-procurement reforms: transparency (Web) and competition; (8) a country diagnostic (and scorecard) on transparency and governance; (9) public disclosure of assets and incomes of candidates, public officials, politicians, legislators, and their dependents; and (10) public disclosure of political campaign contributions by individuals and firms, and of campaign expenditures.

more strategic in ensuring that their equity and lending approaches promote a level playing field in the enterprise sector, rather than supporting and investing in monopolistic forces or elite captors. This would require not only improved due diligence by entities such as the IFC but also a redirection of their strategies, which would become much more supportive of improved governance in the corporate sector and in the private sector–public sector nexus.

• *Support a more decentralized approach, including civil society groups and a multistakeholder national consensus building and action program on political reform.* Beyond the adoption of a basic tenet of not perpetuating autocratic regimes in power by providing large-scale assistance to such central governments, the international community needs to find effective ways of working at a more decentralized level and supporting CSOs and NGOs. Working with CSOs is less controversial today (except in some countries), and many organizations have pronouncements to that effect, but the modalities and priorities remain vague, and the record of agencies having worked at a more decentralized level is spotty.

More specifically, with the rigorous input of in-depth country diagnostics, a multistakeholder group in the country could call for a national forum to discuss an action program of priority governance reforms. Both in action program formulation and in dissemination and implementation, it is important to support the collaborative work of a multistakeholder group of leaders and representatives, namely, in the executive, judiciary, and legislative realms; the private sector; NGOs; and the media—moving away from the previous top-down approach.

- *An illicit and stolen assets initiative.* Substantial capital flight from the Middle East is taking place, some in the form of ill-gotten assets by elites. They are still placed with relative ease in selected safe havens in financial centers, and not merely in the Gulf but also in London, for instance.[11] The international community has a particular responsibility in supporting transition countries to restrict opportunities for asset stripping and theft by significantly tightening their regulations in regard to their own financial centers and in identifying and restituting stolen assets (as has been done in the past in Nigeria, Peru, and Haiti, for example).[12]

It is worth emphasizing that it is a fallacy to have economic and political challenges compete with each other for attention and priority at this juncture of the Arab transition. Both are a priority, partly because they are closely intertwined. Sound economic policies, robust job creation, and shared economic growth will not automatically unfold as a result of technocratic decrees or an infusion of external aid to a government ministry but rather in large measure through improved domestic governance in a number of key dimensions.

---

11 Given the recent tightening of financial regulations in financial centers such as Switzerland, the sense is that London, for instance, is a destination of choice for many such assets.

12 The uneven progress in financial centers' regulatory stance ought to be further examined and taken up more decisively in the context of the Group of Twenty (G20) and other such forums.

INDEX

Abdullah II, 100
Africa, 111, 145
African Union, 16
Algeria
  economic reform, 38
  education, 67
  employment, 18, 43n.10, 56, 58, 92,
    95, 96
  infrastructure, 151, 153n.8, 154
  levels of satisfaction, 51
  manufacturing and industrialization,
    23, 118
  mortgage finance, 90
  political reform, 42n.8
  trade, 109, 144
Arab League, 29, 142
Argentina, 74
Asia, 107, 116, 118, 145, 149
Authoritarian bargain, 18, 32

Bahrain
  education, 60
  employment, 94
  governance, 47, 97
  infrastructure, 154
  political reform, 58
  trade, 148, 150
Banking sector
  access to finance, 111-112

during transition, 20, 85, 107, 158
regional Arab bank, 29, 162
state-owned banks, 85, 111
Bouazizi, Mohammed, 6, 54, 124
Brazil, 16, 48, 113n.7, 160

Central Asia, 49
Chile, 48, 49, 73, 74, 113n.7
China, 113n.7, 118
Civil society
  dialogue with, 16, 26, 27,
    102-103, 104
  and international assistance, 155, 159,
    165, 168, 172
  organizations (CSOs), 6, 73, 99, 102,
    104, 168, 171, 172
  and reform initiatives, 26, 43-44, 73, 99,
    171, 172
  and youth, 6, 27
Credentialism, 19, 62-70
Cronyism, 3, 10, 26, 38, 126, 160, 167

Deauville Partnership, 10, 157n.9, 159
  See also G8
Deauville Summit Declaration, 152
Decentralization, 26, 103, 104, 160
Deregulation, 38, 132
Dubai, 67, 137, 152
Dutch disease, 8, 118, 119, 164